HAREWOOD

Bronze Age to Broadband

HAREWOOD

Bronze Age to Broadband

Professor Jim Maxon

Matador
9 De Montfort Mews
Leicester LE1 7FW, UK
Tel: (+44) 116 255 9311 / 9312
Email: books@troubador.co.uk
Web: www.troubador.co.uk/matador

ISBN 978-1906221-317

Typeset in 11pt Book Antiqua by Troubador Publishing Ltd, Leicester, UK
Printed in the UK by The Cromwell Press Ltd, Trowbridge, Wilts, UK

Matador is an imprint of Troubador Publishing Ltd

Dedication

This book is dedicated to a friend and remarkable woman; a woman who seemed to have adopted the whole village of Harewood; a woman who lived to the age of 95 yet had an active mind of a person half her age; a woman who was the 'grand dame' of the village. The woman was Olive Wild.

Whilst discussing the book with her early in 2006, she gave me some fascinating insights into life in Harewood over the years, and she also showed me her beloved scrapbook about the life and times of HRH Princess Mary (The Princess Royal) that she had kept between the years of 1930 and 1934. At the time, she went on to say that I should feel free to use the contents of this in any way I saw fit.

Olive died just before Christmas 2006. To honour her memory, I decided to edit the scrapbook and to include it as a Chapter in this book. I am quite certain that Olive would be delighted with this and I am sure that you will find it both fascinating and insightful.

Contents

Preface

In many ways I have our neighbours, John and Hilda, to thank for kindling the idea of writing a book about the history of Harewood Village. This came from two questions I asked them during our Christmas drinks chat in 2005: how long had they lived in the village (55 years) and did they know if anyone had written the village's history (not sure). By village standards, John and Hilda are still relative newcomers! Despite this, they were able to regale my wife and I with story upon story of many of the village's 'characters', how the village had changed over time and so on. Not only were we enthralled by what they had to say, they also had us in fits of laughter. Anyway, that is where my interest in this book began.

Given that I have only lived in the village for five years, I believe, strangely enough, that I am just the right person to be writing the book. I have no deep personal history of the village so everything I hear or read is both new and fascinating and I am passionately interested in history. In addition, my academic background has given me a solid foundation in the 'art' of research. I say art rather than science because despite the best attempts of being organised and very painstaking efforts in research methodology, sometimes what you find is pure luck! In other words, for some parts of the book, just about as much information has been gathered via brief chats with my fellow villagers ("Have you talked to X?" or "Have you seen the 'green book'?" type comments) as I am out walking my dog, as has been gathered via searches in Leeds Central Library, the Internet, and so on.

It did not take very long to discover that loads of information had been written about Harewood Village in books, pamphlets, newspaper articles and so on. The problem, as it is with writing any book, is trying to make sense of everything whilst assembling it into a coherent whole and, of course, to write something that is both insightful and interesting to read.

I mentioned earlier that I am passionately interested in history, but I must confess that I find many history books, whether they are about people, places, food, drink, architecture, art or events, are often written in an extremely dull way! I have attempted to rectify that by writing this book in what I hope you will find to be a lively style without demeaning the serious nature of history itself nor losing any of my research credibility and approach.

I hope most sincerely that you enjoy the book, whether you are new to the village or have lived in Harewood all your life, whether you are visiting Harewood House for the first time or are a regular visitor, or perhaps you simply enjoy reading history books.

If you are reading this book but have never visited Harewood, perhaps it will encourage you to do so.

Jim Maxon
Harewood
31st May 2007

Acknowledgements

I would first of all like to express my thanks and gratitude to Lord and Lady Harewood and to David Lascelles for giving me so much of their valuable time during the interviewing process. In addition, I would like to thank Lord and Lady Harewood for providing me with the photograph of themselves and for the wonderful "Foreword" which appears on the back cover.

The second group of people I would like to thank are all those I met with on a one-to-one basis, together with those who sent their fond memory stories or other information to me. They are: Margaret Armstrong, Dr Barbara Brooke, David Copley, Wendy Davey, Sarah Deacon, Ed Dennison (Archive Service), Mrs A Foxcroft, Melissa Gallimore (Harewood House Trust), Hilda Hodgson, Colin Lacey, Nanette Mills, Phyllis Newby, Margaret Trickett, Christopher Ussher and Ethel Wade.

The third group are those who really pulled out the stops to assist me. Dr Barbara Brooke for not only allowing me to interview her, but also letting me take photographs of her Harewood watercolour which features on the front cover of the book. Melissa Gallimore for not only spending time with me being interviewed, but also offering her advice pertaining to contacting the Earl and Viscount, providing information about various activities that have taken place at Harewood House over the years and for also suggesting the name of the photographer who took the watercolour photographs. Also Tony and Carole Dring for the loan of Olive's beloved scrapbook, newspaper articles, books, and so on.

The fourth are the photographer and the map maker for their help and professionalism.

Fifth, John and Hilda for sparking my imagination in the first place that prompted me to write the book.

The sixth group of people are those to whom I have spoken about the book at one time or another who made the 'have you spoken to X?' or 'have you seen the green book?' type of comments, that were also very much appreciated. You might remain anonymous but I would like to thank you just the same.

Finally, I would like to thank my wife Julie, because if it wasn't for her help, support, encouragement, understanding, and proofreading and editing skills, this book would never have become a reality.

Jim Maxon
31st July 2007

Introduction

Harewood is in West Yorkshire and is located almost exactly half way between Leeds and Harrogate on the A61. As places go, Harewood Parish is quite small. However, as you will learn in this book, Harewood used to be much bigger and in bygone times it was a market 'town'. The village could not really be described as pretty or picturesque in that it is not 'twee' with a village green, a village pond, a babbling stream running through it or loads of thatched roofed, rose covered cottages! On the other hand, it does have a great deal of character – the houses are all built of the same Yorkshire stone used in Harewood House and the area is steeped in history. Further, and I guess I am just a bit biased; it has one of the best views over Yorkshire there is! The reason for this, and why Harewood Castle was built here, is that the village is on a hill 100 metres above the beautiful valley of the River Wharfe.

In many ways, the best place to get a 'sampler' taste of the views to be had, is to walk along the bridle-path, an extension of Church Lane which, by the way, is part of the Ebor Way. Although the start of the walk is through a walled and heavily wooded area, it soon opens up to give some stunning views of the Wharfe valley. If you stop for a moment, just before crossing the cattle grid, you will be rewarded with wonderful views of the hills of North Yorkshire, including Almscliff Crag (a large outcrop of Millstone Grit), the majestic spire of St Barnabas Church in Weeton (built in 1851 and paid for by the Earl of Harewood), some glimpses of the River Wharfe itself, including the site of an ancient castle at Rougemont (a large green wood on the bend of the river) plus the Wharfedale Viaduct near Arthington (for those who are interested, the viaduct carries the railway over the River Wharfe, was completed in 1849, is 460 metres long, has 21 rounded arches, and yes, it is the same viaduct that appears at the beginning of *Emmerdale*!). So, it is not just the stunning views that attract people to this particular walk, nor the chance to see red and roe deer or the abundant other wildlife including red kites, but also because of people's interest in seeing the area in which *Emmerdale* is filmed!

After drinking in the lovely views before the cattle grid, you might be tempted to turn left and walk up the short path to the ancient churchyard of All Saints Church. Also, if you cross over the cattle grid, stop immediately and look directly North into the valley, you will see Harewood Bridge.

Obviously, there is far, far more to Harewood than the stunning views and the chance to have a fine walk around the Harewood House estate, including the impact that 'Capability' Brown had on the area. It is an area steeped in history that is not only interesting, it is riveting!

To help you to find most of the names of places, extinct villages, routes and so on, that are mentioned throughout this book, a map of the area follows this Introduction.

The picture on the front cover of the book is a watercolour by Walter Cecil Horsnell. He was a well-known landscape artist who faithfully recorded the charming rural scenes whilst travelling through Yorkshire in the 1950s. The watercolour captures a bygone Harewood, as seen looking North towards Harrogate. Although the watercolour has no date, it was obviously painted prior to 1962, as in that year the gales destroyed the fine elm trees shown in the picture. The original water-colour is owned by Dr Barbara Brooke and I am very grateful to her for allowing me to take pictures of this wonderful watercolour. The pictures were actually taken by Norman Taylor, a commercial and industrial photographer who has, over the years, taken many photographs of the artwork contained in the Harewood House collection.

The book is written in the first person and throughout the book I have made use of both footnotes and endnotes within each Chapter. Footnotes offer additional information pertaining to a particular item within the main body of the text whilst endnotes show the relevant references for quoted works (within the endnotes, 'ibid' means the refer-ence immediately before and 'op cit' means a previously referenced work, which is not immediately before).

Two final points to note. Firstly, Henry Lascelles bought the manor of Harewood from the Boulter family who were forced by debt to sell the estate. John Boulter died in 1738 and whilst the Harewood website and *Harewood: A Guide* state that the manor was sold to Lascelles in the same year, most historians give the date as 1739. I have therefore used this date throughout the book. Secondly, I make no claim that the index is exhaustive, but I have included what I consider to be key links to infor-mation within the book.

Map of Harewood and Surrounding Area

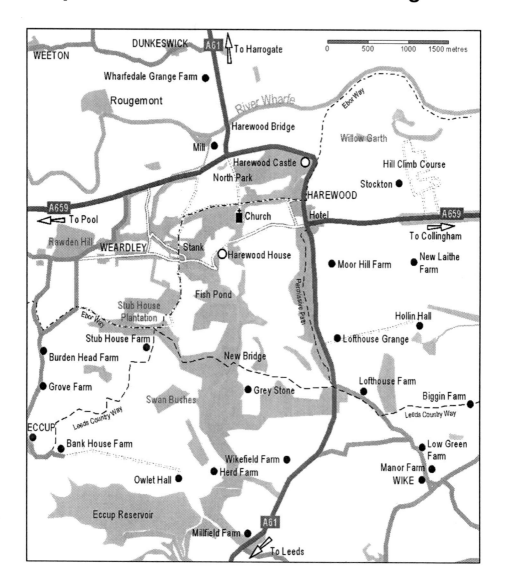

This map was redrawn by Customised Mapping from printed Ordnance Survey mapping Crown Copyright©. Please note that the representation of any road, track or path is no evidence of the existence of a right of way. In addition, information is shown subject to the limitations of the scale of mapping.

CHAPTER ONE

Harewood Before 1066

Grey Stone with Harewood House in the distance

Introduction

I have to confess that when I started my initial research, I had no idea what evidence actually existed in terms of the historical origins of Harewood. I was delighted to discover that there was convincing evidence of links as far back as the Bronze Age (and probably even to Prehistoric times). Ideas for the title of the book quickly followed!

Bronze Age and Earlier

Before going on to give details of the evidence of Bronze Age links to Harewood, I feel I need to say something about the term Bronze Age.

1

According to an on-line encyclopaedia called Wikipedia, "the Bronze Age is a period in a civilisation's development when the most advanced metal working consisted of techniques for smelting copper and tin from naturally occurring outcroppings of ore, and then alloying those metals in order to cast bronze". In Great Britain, the Bronze Age is considered to have been the period from around 2100 to 500 BC. Being more precise than that in terms of 'Age' is a bit tricky because whether it be the Stone Age prior to the Bronze Age, or the Iron Age that follows, 'Age' refers to the development of the people in a particular area rather than a specific time. In other words, the Stone Age refers to the time before people started using bronze and the Bronze Age refers to a time when people were using bronze rather than iron. As people developed, they switched, gradually, from using old materials such as stone, to the newly 'invented' bronze or copper for making the implements they needed for survival or basic living – cooking, hunting, for decorations, things they buried with their dead and so on. Therefore, because of the gradual change in 'technology' over time, archaeologists are sometimes uncertain as to the exact date of a particular site because they might very well find stone implements in what is regarded to be a Bronze Age site, and the manner in which people were buried is not always definitive because burial traditions also changed gradually over time.

I am extremely grateful to Christopher Ussher, Resident Agent at Harewood Estate, for providing me with details of *The Heritage Plan* – an historical assessment of Harewood undertaken by the Estate. The purpose of this had been to establish the archaeological and historical past of the Harewood Estate in order to understand the origins of the present landscape vis-à-vis the landscape at various times in the past. Evidence was gathered from documentary and archival research, site surveys, and interviews with local residents and Harewood staff. This research indicated that Harewood's history may actually date as far back as the Prehistoric Period (approximately 3000 BC)!

The picture that emerges from the data provided by the document, *The Heritage Plan*[i], is that Harewood "may have provided good hunting grounds with woods, valleys and streams able to support a large population of deer in the early days of human occupation".

High on the skyline above Grey Stone Pasture, on the Harewood Estate, is a large boulder known as Grey Stone. This is, according to the *Heritage Plan*, a "large glacial erratic boulder of Millstone Grit" bearing various markings "which are believed to date from the Late Neolithic and Bronze Age periods (2800 BC to 500 BC)". According to the website fettes.com, an *erratic* is a

boulder transported and deposited by a glacier which is different in compo-
sition from the rocks upon which it is sitting. Millstone Grit is made of
sandstone and is common in this part of Yorkshire. Although no other
erratics are believed to exist on the Harewood Estate, they are very common
throughout the United Kingdom, including the Lake District, as mentioned
in one of William Wordsworth's poems[1].

> "As a huge Stone is sometimes seen to lie
> Couched on the bald top of an eminence;
> Wonder to all who do the same espy,
> By what means it could thither come, and whence;
> So that it seems a thing endued with sense:
> Like a Sea-beast crawled forth, that on a shelf
> Of rock or sand reposeth, there to sun itself."

There is no doubt that Grey Stone could be described as Wordsworth has,
especially when you are looking up to it from the path between New Bridge
and the Lofthouse Gates (along the Leeds Country Way[2]).

The potential importance of Grey Stone in terms of the name "Harewood" is
explored further in Chapter Two.

An arrowhead flint was found near Lofthouse and Neolithic and Mesolithic
flints have also been found on the grounds of the Estate. Furthermore, an
early Bronze Age perforated axe hammer was ploughed up at Biggin Farm.

The Heritage Plan gives additional Bronze Age evidence with reference to a
Bronze Age trade route from Ireland to Scandinavia, which is said to have
passed between Otley and Tadcaster, going through, or near to, Harewood.
Such routes would have run along or close to the River Wharfe whilst
scattered farmsteads may have been built on drier ground above.

The evidence offered indicates an obvious link between Biggin Farm,
Lofthouse and Grey Stone and if you look at the map you will see that all
three appear on a walk (the Leeds Country Way). If one continues past Grey
Stone, the walk will eventually merge with the Ebor Way. The Ebor Way is a
112 km/70 miles walk that runs from Helmsley to Ilkley passing through

---

1. The poem, written in 1802, was known as *The Leech Gatherer* before publication but was subse-
    quently called *Resolution and Independence*.
2. The Leeds Country Way is a 62 mile circular walk around greater Leeds and Harewood falls
    within it.

York, Tadcaster, Wetherby and Harewood. This would certainly indicate to me that this is part of the Ireland to Scandinavia Bronze Age trade route referred to earlier.

The Roman Period

As mentioned in *The Heritage Plan,* there was certainly a Roman road running East-West through Ilkley, Adel and Tadcaster which passed close to the Southern edge of the present Harewood Estate. There was a Romano-British settlement in Adel and a Roman fort in Tadcaster. Near Biggin Farm a coin hoard was found which is thought to date from the 1st or 2nd Century. Archaeological evidence suggests there may well have been a Roman villa at Biggin Farm, since roofing and *hypocaust* tiles, a *stone capital*, stone guttering, *querns*, and mainly 4th Century pottery have been found there. (For the non archaeologists amongst us, a *hypocaust* is a hollow space under the floor in ancient Roman houses, into which hot air was sent for heating a room or bath.[3] A *stone capital* is carved decorative stonework that appears at the top of a column or above a door. *Querns* are stone hand-mills used for grinding corn.) In addition, a Roman altar was found nearby at Wike in 1864.

The Angles and the Brigantes

Wade[ii] wrote that "being on the northern border of the ancient and independent Kingdom of Elmete, Harewood no doubt suffered when King Edwin[4] conquered these lands about 620 AD, and the area was to be populated by the Angles. Once, too, Harewood had been in the Kingdom of Northumbria and, earlier still, was land of the Brigantes[5] whose domain extended into Cumbria, Lancashire and towards East Riding".

A website called geocities.com, created by Tim Midgley, highlighted some fascinating facts about the Kingdom of Elmete. Elmete was an independent British kingdom in the 400s-600s AD and was situated in what are now

---

3.   *The Concise Oxford Dictionary* (1990).
4.   Edwin annexed the minor British kingdom of Elmete on the death of its King Ceretic in 617. Ceretic, born in about 560, was the last King of Elmet. He died defending his kingdom against the invading Northumbrians. King Edwin of Deira had just reclaimed his kingdom after years in exile. He re-asserted himself on Northern Britain by invading first Bernicia and then Elmet.
5.   The Brigantes were a tribe – or perhaps more accurately a loose confederation of related tribes – of British Celts inhabiting almost all of the area between the Humber and the Tyne. The name of the tribe springs from the Celtic goddess Brigantia. At the time of the Roman invasion in 43 AD the Brigantes were arguably the most powerful Celtic tribe in Britain.

parts of North, West and South Yorkshire. According to the website, "Elmet (Elmed/Elfed) called *Elmete Saetan* or the 'dwelling place of the people of Elmete' came into prominence following the evacuation of the Roman Legions from Britain after 407-410 AD." In terms of the origin of Elmete, it is believed that the Celtic-British Brigantes had revolted against the Romans in 155 AD, burning down the fort at Ilkley (Olicana), however they were soon overcome and the fort was re-built. The article went on to say that "it is likely that at this time the local Romano-Celtic British tribes in the vicinity of Leeds (Loidis) separated from the Brigantes and formed an alliance with the Romans. The Romans found it convenient to rule by alliances with local chiefs. The local tribes formed themselves into the Kingdom of Elmet."

The Anglo-Saxon Period

The Heritage Plan pointed out that "after a period of Anglo-Saxon occupation, Harewood would have fallen under the Danelaw in 876 AD when York was occupied by the Danish army". It went on to say that "the area was then invaded by the Scandinavians from Dublin, and did not return to Anglo-Saxon rule until Eric 'Bloodaxe' was driven out in 955 AD". The Harewood area is called 'Skyrack Wapentake' which is Scandinavian for 'shire-oak'. For information, Eric Bloodaxe was the second king of Norway from 930 to 934 AD and lived from c. 885 to 955 AD. Many historians believe that the 'blood' part of his nickname came from the fact that as a result of quarrelling with his brothers, he had four of them killed.

Place names from between the 7th and 10th Centuries have survived to this day. For example, Dunkeswick and East Keswick are derived from the Anglo-Saxon word 'keswick' which means 'cheese farm' and suggest dairy farming on the flood plain of the River Wharfe. Lofthouse, Stainburn and Kearby are Old Norse names. Weardley is derived from Old English and means 'Wigferth's forest glade' – according to *The Heritage Plan*.

The final pieces of information that *The Heritage Plan* had to offer for this period was that "this scatter of settlements indicates that the landscape was fully settled. A reference to Farmon[6], the priest of Harewood in the late 9th Century shows that a religious focus had appeared there". A fragment of a cross shaft which was found at Harewood Church (All Saints) is believed to be of Anglo-Scandinavian origin of the 10th or 11th Century. This fragment is on display within All Saints Church.

---

6.   Additional information about this 9th Century priest is contained in Chapter Three.

Further information pertaining to the Anglo-Saxon period in the life of Harewood, comes from the unpublished work of Dennison and Richardson[iii]. In their writing, quoting from Faull (1981), they stated that "a late Anglo-Saxon coin hoard, comprising 30 coins and two half cut pennies of Edward the Confessor[7], was found in 1895 close to the gate leading to the West end of Harewood Church and a series of earthworks to the North-East of the Church may represent the site of an Anglo-Saxon settlement" (Faull 1981, 187 & 194). Dennison and Richardson concluded that the evidence available suggests that the wider parish of Harewood originated as an important Anglo-Saxon estate with a valuable ecclesiastical centre and which was also based on dairy farming.

Harewood Fables

Dennison and Richardson[iv] mentioned that according to Jewell (1819), approximately half a mile West of the Castle, within West End wood, there used to be an open space known as 'Chasne Plain', that had been kept clear of trees for many years, which allegedly marked the place where King Edgar murdered the Earl Aethelwold in 963 AD. In researching this further, I discovered that later historians, whilst not dismissing that the event actually happened, believe that the Harewood in which this killing took place was not, in fact, this Harewood but one in the South of the country. The general view is that the event took place in Whorwell in Hampshire.

In gathering research for this book I unearthed a fascinating story in the January 1938 edition of the *Harewood News.*

> "Once upon a time, a certain Giant lived on Ilkley Moor. From this vantage point, on a clear morning, he used to be able to see right across the vale of York. However, one fine day, he awoke to find his view obscured by the newly built York Minster. The Giant was not unnaturally rather peeved at this outrage. Retaliation seemed essential. So, picking up two of the rather large pebbles which lie ready to hand on Ilkley Moor, he hurled them at the cause of his wrath. But he had considerably overestimated his throwing-powers, for one of the stones landed at Almscliff and the other on Grey Stone Hill in Harewood Park."

---

7. Edward III (the Confessor) was the eldest son of Ethelred II and was the penultimate Anglo-Saxon king. The last Anglo-Saxon king was Harold Godwinson who became Harold II upon the death of Edward.

The article went on to say that when Mr John Jones, author of *The History and Antiquities of Harewood* (1859) was told the story he said "this legend *cannot* however be believed!" Given that Mr Jones lived in the middle of the 19th Century, it seems that this legend has been part of Harewood's folklore for a very long time.

From the Anglo-Saxon period we move on to the next Chapter which picks up Harewood's story from 1066.

End Notes

i   Harewood Estate, *The Heritage Plan*, Private Document.

ii   Ron Wade, *Vat Sal Be Sal* (1982), p 2.

iii   Ed Dennison and S Richardson, *Harewood Castle, Harewood, West Yorkshire: An Archaeological and Architectural Condition Survey* (unpublished EDAS report for Harewood Estate) (forthcoming), p 1.

iv   Ibid, p 1.

CHAPTER TWO
Harewood 1066 to 2007

Harewood Chapel and Post Office

Introduction

In 1859 Jones[i] described Harewood as follows:

> "The Village of Harewood is pleasantly situated on the Leeds and Harrogate Road, about 8 miles distant from each town. The history of the village of Harewood is, in a great measure, connected with the history of its lords and castle. Its position is one of great beauty, standing on a considerable eminence overlooking the valley of the Wharfe. To the West a prospect of a most diversified character presents itself embracing the magnificent scenery of Wharfedale, for nearly 20 miles, bounded in the distance by the hills of Craven; while to the East the Vale of York lays stretched out before the observer, York Minister being clearly

discernible at the distance of 20 miles. Standing at the intersection of two high roads; the great North Road and the highway from the West to York, it was formerly a place of much life and bustle, twenty two stage coaches passing and repassing every day. The introduction of the railroads however destroyed this traffic. The cottages are erected uniformly on these two roads, and most of them having gardens in the front, under the shade of fine trees, the traveller or visitor is generally struck with the regularity and beauty of the village."

In some ways, much has changed in the village since Jones wrote these words almost 150 years ago. More houses being built, the destruction of the fine elms on The Avenue and Harrogate Road by disease and the great gale of 1962[1], and virtually all of the local shops disappearing, are just a few examples. Despite these, however, much of the character of the village survives, including many houses designed by the famous architect John Carr, All Saints Church (with its Norman font and medieval tombs), the remains of the Castle, and, in addition, the vistas from the village remain the same as they always have been.

There are, of course, slightly different ways of describing Harewood. "This is the neatest village in the county, the houses of which are uniformly and handsomely built of stone, consisting of two streets, one running North and South, the other East and West, the latter forming a regular approach to the gateway leading to Harewood House; and the houses have, at first view, more the appearance of habitations of gentlemen than tenantry."[ii] Dr Whitaker[2] (as quoted by Jewell – 1819) has a slightly different take. "This is a fortunate place, blessed with much natural beauty and fertility, and, in the compass of a country village, with an entire though dismantled Castle, a modern palace surrounded by a wide extent of pleasure grounds and plantations, and a Parish Church filled with unmutilated sculptures of the fourteenth and fifteenth centuries."[iii]

What's in a name?

Before moving on to discuss Harewood from the beginning of its recorded history in 1066, I think it is best to get two things out of the way first – where

---

1.   Apparently, the tall elms almost formed a complete arch when the trees were in full summer foliage. The 1962 gale also decimated 'Capability' Brown's woodscape around Harewood House.

2.   Dr Whitaker, author of the *History of Craven*, is an often quoted historian by eminent historians themselves, Jewell and Griffith.

did the name Harewood come from and is it pronounced Harwood or Harewood? Dr Whitaker claimed that the name came from the abundance of hares in the area. Nonsense, say other historians. The ancient spelling of the village was 'Herawudu' which undoubtedly meant the wood of the 'Herr', the owner or proprietor, and this term was commonly used in Anglo-Saxon times. The Herr or Hera who gave the name to the hamlet may have been an early thane[3] who owned the forest and built his stronghold on the hill where now stands the ruin of Harewood Castle. Other thoughts on the origin of the name of Harewood came from Wade[iv] when he mentioned that

> "Haer meant a temple in a wood; Heres were ancient soldiers. Har was a defensive position or place for soldiers and other examples of this are HARtlepool, HARwich and, more locally HARlow Hill, meaning Here-low – a soldier's hill. Wode, to become wood, could have been the dye, woad, with which the ancient Britons daubed themselves; wood may be related to Harewood being on the edge of Knaresborough Forest; or, perhaps, from wada (water or to wade) – and isn't the Wharfe nearby?"

Smith[v], on the other hand, mentioned that the name Harewood may also have come from the word 'haer' which he defined as Old English for 'rock or heap of stones' or possibly from 'Grey Stone Wood' or 'Grey Stone' (from 'hara' meaning grey).

Therefore, many historians have offered perfectly feasible suggestions as to where the name came from. However, Smith's is, to me, the most likely. The reason why I am convinced that he is correct is the fact that Grey Stone, mentioned in the last Chapter, has been in existence, and therefore known about, for somewhere between 2,500 and 4,500 years. How much more logical can it be than to name a place after an object that is a dominant feature on the skyline. From Grey Stone one has commanding views over Harewood House, towards the River Wharfe and to the Craven Hills. It is easy to imagine Grey Stone being a well-known meeting place for many millennia.

Anyway, the property of 19 square miles that Robert de Romelli was given after the Conquest was known as Harwode. It was also known as Hoorewood, Harwod and Harwud. The different spellings could be attributed to the mix of languages associated with the people who lived in the

---

3.   Thane is a man who held land from an English king or other superior by military service, ranking between ordinary freemen and hereditary nobles. (*The Concise Oxford Dictionary*)

area at the time – the Angles, the Saxons and the Danes. I have to say I also agree with Wade[vi] that illiteracy at the time may have contributed to the different spellings!

There has always been controversy regarding the proper pronunciation of the name Harewood, some insisting that it is pronounced as written, others that the first syllable should rhyme with 'bar'. It has also been said that pronouncing Harewood as Harwood was a Southern affectation! The letter 'e' first appeared in about the mid-1700s and seems to coincide with the first Lascelles becoming Lord of the Manor. It is reported that when the 6th Lord Harewood became engaged to the Princess Mary in November 1921, members of the press asked him the correct pronunciation of his name – he stated that it was Harwood, and not Harewood. Furthermore, in 1937, when the Earl, who was then the Provincial Grand Master of a Masonic Lodge (he became Grand Master in 1942), was approached to ask if the Branch could be called "Harewood Lodge", apparently the Earl granted this wish with the proviso that it should always be pronounced "Harwood" and never "Harewood"!

So despite the fact that the 6th Earl seems to have sorted the pronunciation out many years ago, the village remains 'schizophrenic' in that it lives with two names! Most of the locals, including the majority of people who live in Yorkshire, not just villagers, call it *Hare*wood whilst people answering the phone at Harewood House will say, "hello, this is *Har*wood".

1066 and all that

"At the time of the Norman Conquest in 1066, Harewood as recorded in the Domesday Book (1086) seems to have belonged to Tor, Sprot and Grim, three Saxon Chieftains, who as supporters of Earl Morcar (the Earl of Northumbria from 1065 to 1066) were dispossessed by the new King, their lands passing into his domain."[vii] William the Conqueror replaced Morcar with Robert Comine as the Earl of Northumbria. Morcar had been at the very heart of events leading the great battles of 1066 and the resistance movement that failed to prevent or reverse the Norman Conquest of Anglo-Saxon England. After the defeat of King Harold at Hastings, Morcar became the leader of the English resistance movement until he was eventually captured at the battle of Ely and imprisoned, where he died in 1071. The resistance movement did not die with Morcar but went on until 1088. Many people have the false belief that Anglo-Saxon England simply became Anglo-Norman England when Harold was killed in Hastings in 1066. Much to the annoyance of William, the Anglo-Saxons did not give in without a significant and prolonged fight!

William was extremely generous to one of his supporters, Robert de Romelli (also known as de Rumilly) of Skipton Castle. He belonged to an important family in Normandy (land of the Northmen) who came to England with William. The rewards for Romelli's support included Harewood in 1094. At the time of Domesday, Harewood manor alone comprised eight townships (Harewood, Alwoodley, East Keswick, Weardley, Wigton, Wike, Dunkeswick and Weeton). According to Kennedy,[viii]

> "so well cultivated was the land that more than two out of every three acres was bearing crops. It was one of the richest manorial prizes in England. Not surprisingly, Robert's only daughter Cecily made a good marriage with the Earl of Chester, William de Meschines, who brought with him a substantial slice of Cumberland to add to the Harewood estates. (Henry I granted the family all the land lying between the rivers Duddon and Derwent and between the lakes of Bassenthwaite and Derwentwater)".

One of the daughters of this marriage, Avicia, married William de Curci (also shown as de Curcy), Steward to the Household of Henry I. It was this William de Curci who founded Harewood Church (All Saints) in 1116.

From 1066 to the 19th Century

The village probably reached its high point in the early 13th Century as a result of being granted a Charter by King John in 1209, the 10th year of his reign. The Charter was granted to Warin Fitz Gerald, his chamberland, (sometimes shown as Fitz-Gerold or Waryn Fitz Gerald or Warren Fitzgerald), who by his marriage to Alicia (or Alice) de Curci, granddaughter of Avicia and William de Curci, became Lord of the Manor.

A translation of the Charter to Warin Fitz Gerald by King John in 1209 states:

> "John, by the Grace of God, &c. Know ye that we have granted, and so by this charter confirm to Warin Fitz Gerald and to his heirs, the possession of one warren[4] at Harwood, in the county of York, and to hold one fair there every year, to continue for

---

4.   According to Kennedy, a 'free warren' is the granting of the sole right to kill game on the estate, which would otherwise have been considered royal property under the forest laws dating from the Norman Conquest.

three days, to wit, on the first day of July and the two following days, and also to hold one market there every week on the Monday, yet so that the aforesaid fair and market do in no wise interfere with the neighbouring fairs and neighbouring markets. Wherefore our will and pleasure is, that the aforesaid Warin and his heirs have and hold in their aforesaid manor of Harwood, the aforesaid warren, with the liberties and free customs pertaining to a warren of this kind, and the aforesaid fair and market well and peaceably, freely and quietly, with all the liberties and free customs belonging to our town of Richmond as is aforesaid. Given by the hand of Henry de Wells, Archdeacon of Wells, at Lambeth, the 16th day of February, in the 10th year of our reign."[ix]

Dennison and Richardson[x], in making reference to both information from the Harewood Estate and Harewood House Trust, and that of Parker (1913), mentioned that when Fitzgerald was granted free warren of the manor of Harewood in c. 1209, it is likely that the area around the Castle was enclosed and was shown as 'Castle Park' on later maps.

The Charter seems to have been renewed at various times. In 1407 Sir Richard Redman obtained a grant for a fair and free warren in Harewood; in 1445 Sir William Ryther got a patent for a market, fair, and free warren in Harewood; and in 1633 Lord Strafford obtained a confirmation of all these previous grants. The market, however, seems to have stopped before 1570.

According to Buckle[xi]

"the main portion of the town was centred on the Wetherby Road (opposite the present main gates of Harewood House). This road was on an incline from the Leeds/Harrogate road and was only levelled in the early part of the nineteenth Century. This accounts for the gardens of the estate houses on the left being much higher than the road. On this site stood the town's hall, which was in effect a market house and toll booth. Some idea of the size of the town can be judged by the fact that there were six butchers' shops underneath the market house. Outside this building were the village stocks and pillory, and close to the toll booth was a strong ring fastened to a large stone where the villagers enjoyed the sport of bull-baiting or bear-baiting."

Jones[xii] speculated that the market or town's hall was pulled down around the year 1656, although he said that the exact date was not known. Wade[xiii] on the other hand, stated that the building, also referred to as "a large Toll Booth or Court House with shambles underneath" was pulled down c. 1768. If this is the same building, it is not clear why there are 112 years between the two dates!

In further describing the layout of the village, Buckle[xiv] stated that "in the centre of this road, about fifty yards higher up than the town was the Market Cross. This consisted of a large stone pedestal with a quadrangular flight of seven very broad steps on which the neighbouring farmers and their wives stood to sell their butter, eggs, poultry, etc."

One of the greatest alterations in the village, according to Jones, were the roads, although Buckle's[xv] description of the roads is more accurate.

> "The Leeds/Harrogate Turnpike Road turned to the left just beyond the present entrance gate to the House and passed into the Square with Moor House[5] on the right, and continued past the Coach Road with its Lodge, which was the original entrance to the House, along the side of the Plantation, followed the Tadcaster and Otley Turnpike Road for a short distance then turned right and descended the hill to the bridge, near to the old Toll Bar. This road ran through the North Park past the quarry, and near to the curve stood another toll bar, which in 1753 was the scene of a riot which arose out of the discontent and opposition to the Turnpike Act." (See separate section for the Turnpike Riots.)

The Market Cross, mentioned above, was re-erected in 1703 by John Boulter but in 1804, when the road was lowered, it was taken down and destroyed. An unusual feature of this cross was that on top of the upright was a knor and spell, a game for which the village was once celebrated. According to the *Dictionary of Phrase and Fable*, 1898, by E Cobham Brewer,

> "nurr and spell or knor and spill is a game resembling trapball, a game played with a trap, and is played with a wooden ball called a nurr or knor. The ball is released by means of a spring from a little brass cup at the end of a tongue of steel called a *spell* or *spill*. After the player has touched the spring, the ball flies into the air, and is struck with a bat. In scoring, the distances are reckoned by the

---

5.   Moor House was formerly the Estate Office.

score feet, previously marked off by a Gunter's chain. A Gunter's chain is also known as a survey chain and is 4 poles or 66 feet."

It is clear that the village that the Lascelles moved into in 1739 would have been a prosperous market town.

In the middle of the 18th Century there were six public houses in the village, the White Hart (Lodge Green), Black Bull (near the Square), Shoulder of Mutton (above the Vicarage), Red Lion (near the Square), Crown (at the bottom of the town), Star Inn (in Bondgate) and one at the Bridge. Having said that, many would have been little more than a room dedicated to drinking within a private house, not as we would perceive them based on how a typical pub is today.

In the late 18th Century and early 19th Century Harewood must have been a hive of activity. For example, the village was being rebuilt in keeping with the classic architecture of Carr's and Adam's mansion – Harewood House. Given the extensive rebuilding of the village over time, it is not at all surprising that historians have had great difficulty in trying to find the exact dates of the re-building of Harewood village. The situation is, of course, not helped by the fact that very, very few buildings within the village have the date of building inscribed somewhere on them, usually on the door lintel. [There are two notable exceptions – Ivy Cottage (1675) and Cutler's Cottage owned by John Cutler (1678)]. In addition, most historians thought that the old village of Gawthorpe, clustered around the Church, was moved several hundred yards as the park of Harewood House was extended, thus becoming part of Harewood village. In Kennedy's[xvi] book she pointed out that

> "in May 1962 students of Leeds University on a fieldwork course based on the Harewood archives concluded not only that the rebuilding took place later than usually supposed, somewhere between 1796 and 1812, but that the village layout had changed very little over the centuries. By comparing maps made around 1690, 1796, 1812 and 1850, they found no evidence that it had ever encircled the church. However, the gale of 1962 had brought down many 150 year old trees on the north side of Church Lane, revealing large masses of worked stone among the tree roots. This confirmed that houses had once stood there, though they do not appear on the 1812 map, so these villagers may have been moved in the rebuilding. On the whole, however, the students concluded that the pre-Carr village of 1690 was not unlike that of

today in its layout; there was a scatter of houses south of the castle where the medieval bondmen had lived (the terrace is still known as Bondgate) and a symmetrical line of houses corresponding to the present Avenue. There had also been houses on the western side of the Leeds road which were evidently pulled down to make room for the park extension and the buildings of the Doric arch entrance[6], designed by Carr and executed in 1801 by John Muschamp, the village mason."

Although the new houses in the village were very small, (most were only four rooms), the approach that Carr took, in the mid 18th Century, was really rather clever. The new houses were built directly behind the existing ones and when the new houses were completed, people moved from old to new. The old one was then removed and a long front garden created between the new house and the road (The Avenue).

According to Jewell,[xvii] "Harewood may be distinguished from almost every other village in the kingdom, by its regularity and neatness . . . (it) has been uniformly and modestly rebuilt, so as to exclude every appearance of filth or poverty". "The whole of the town is built with fine stone, procured from the neighbouring quarries, and even the cottages possess a look of neatness bordering upon elegance." He was describing the small houses in terraces along the re-aligned turnpike road from Leeds to Harrogate, and on the South side of The Avenue, the road from Collingham to the entrance to Harewood House. It seems that the description of the village by Jewell reflected the original intention of Lascelles when he was reputed to have said to his architects, "let us do everything properly and well, mais pas trop".

The creation of the new houses, along with the ribbon factory (which has also been called the silk factory), marked a major turning point in the history of the village. Edwin Lascelles built the ribbon factory in 1755 as an attempt to add more employment to the area. However, despite his best intentions, the village remained tied to the land. According to Jewell, the ribbon factory discontinued after about eleven years, when labour became scarce, and the factory was closed. The factory building, on the North side of The Avenue, with its distinctive half-moon-shaped upper windows became four cottages, and remains the same today. The other way that the Harewood Estate attempted to bring non-agricultural investment into the

---

6.   A Doric Arch is typically a grand, imposing entrance. The word Doric comes from the name of the fluted pilaster columns. Another Doric Arch is Marble Arch in London, built by John Nash in 1828. It was the chief entrance to Buckingham Palace until the Palace was extended in 1851 and now stands as an entrance to Hyde Park and near Oxford Street.

area was, according to Walvin[xviii], an experiment in the extraction of coal back in the 18th Century. Unfortunately, Walvin did not mention when the experiment took place, where it took place (apart from somewhere on the Harewood Estate) or how successful it was.

There is a lovely little story written about a trip by Reverend Ismay to 'Chapel Allerton and Harwood' in 1767.[xix]

> "Harwood is a pretty little Town, where there is a costly stone Bridge of 11 Arches[7] over the River Wherfe, which runs in a bed of stone, and looks as clear as rock-water. Here aree ye ruins of a Castle. The Church is remarkable for ye Interrment of Sir William Gascoigne, who had the courage to commit Prince Henry, afterwards King Henry 5th to ye King's Bench for affronting him in ye seat of Justice. We called upon Mr Saml. Popplewel, Steward to Edwin Lascelles Esqr.[8] and his two brothers, Daniel and Edward."

> "Mr P. prevailed upon us to alight and take a Glass of his fine Ale. He gave us a note to Mr Hutton ye Gardener at Gawthorpe, who was very obliging in shewing us everything that was curious in the Gardens, stoves and Fire walls. The new House of Edwin Lascelles, Esq. at Gawthorpe is a very noble and elegant structure, but not quite finished.[9] It measured 97 yards in length, stands on an Eminence near the Church and makes a grand appearance. The stables are near ye old House, and are very beautiful. The Gardens are situate upon a large piece of rising Ground in the Valley below, almost surrounded with swamps and Marshes, which are designed to be laid under Water."

Methodism was in existence in the village as early as 1772, the services being held in private houses. According to Wade, E[xx] the homes belonged to William Pool, William Thomas and Edmund Parker. She went on to say that

---

7. Perhaps the Reverend Ismay's notes were interpreted incorrectly or Mr Popplewel's 'fine ale' was far too strong, but the current Harewood Bridge, built in 1729, definitely has only four arches and not eleven.

8. Near the West door of Harewood Church is an inscription to Samuel and Sarah Popplewell, late of Harewood. He died on September 22nd 1780 aged 67 having continued over thirty years as steward to Mr Edwin Lascelles, later the first Lord Harewood (*History and Antiquities of Harewood*, Jones, 1859, p 127)

9. The present Harewood House, begun in 1759, was completed in 1771. Ismay's visit was to Gawthorpe, the house standing less than 400 yards to the South West of the present mansion, the earlier home of the Redmans, the Gascoignes and the Wentworths. It was pulled down after the completion of the new building, no traces of either the house or the neighbouring village surviving (Jones, Ibid., pp 185, 199)

"the first Methodist Chapel, having a high room and a balcony, adapted from two cottages on the north side of The Avenue, was opened in the latter months of 1815. The property had been granted by the 2nd Earl of Harewood. Services took place here until transferred to premises adjoining the Post Office in 1964". The dedication service for this new Chapel took place at 4pm on 22nd April 1964. The site Ethel referred to is the current Anglican-Methodist Chapel. The first Chapel was at 5 The Avenue.

It was not just the Methodists who were active in Harewood, as Buckle[xxi] mentioned that in "1740 the house of William Wright in Lofthouse, in the parish of Harewood, was Registered in the Registry of the Archbishop of York as a place of religious worship for the people called Quakers". Their burial ground was at East Keswick.

The medieval feel to the village including the bear-baiting ring and the stocks were removed in the early 19th Century. Another aspect of the village that changed at about the same time is the village pond. Even stranger than filling in a village pond is where it actually was. According to Kennedy[xxii], it was on the North side of The Avenue but in a painting by John Varley on page 11 of *Harewood: A Guide*, the village pond appears to be on the South side! Although several historians make play of the fact that at one time Harewood village had many pubs – as mentioned above – Harewood's first, and only, real pub and inn, the Harewood Arms, was built in 1810. According to a guidebook of the time, mentioned in the Kennedy book, the Harewood Arms was 'fitted up in a neat and commodious manner' and 'the rooms are well furnished with new beds and bedding, the cellars are well stored with liquors; good post-chaise, able horses, and careful drivers are at command.'

According to Buckle[xxiii], Harewood and its immediate area has always been regarded as having pure and bracing air, and this no doubt accounted for the longevity of its inhabitants, many of whom were close to a hundred years old when they died. Records from the middle of the 19th Century showed that there were at that time a considerable number of octogenarians in the village. Although the air is still bracing, given the amount of traffic along the very busy A61 and the A659, I suspect that it is far from the pure air described in Buckle's guide!

Also in the 19th Century it was recorded that the houses were well supplied with water which was brought from Hollin Hall (close to Lofthouse Grange on the map) to the reservoir near Stockton. This had been constructed by the Earl of Harewood for the benefit of the villagers, and added to Harewood's reputation as a model village.

The school with two houses for teachers which had been erected about 1768 by Edwin Lascelles, was replaced in 1845 by the 3rd Earl of Harewood, the Countess at the time supplied all the books and equipment. The main school hall, which could accommodate about three hundred was used as the village hall, and meetings and lectures were held there. Thoresby[10] mentions that John Boulter[11] founded an earlier school but there are no records of this, and earlier James Ryther[12] had attempted to establish 'a free skoole and releefe of the poore w'in the parish and mannor of Harwode'.

At a meeting presided over by the Earl of Harewood, in March 1853, a Literary and Scientific Institute was formed next to the Village Shop and Post Office, with the object of providing a Reading Room, Library, Lectures, Evening Classes and Branch Libraries.[13] Lectures were given every fortnight from October until April and were well attended. The library flourished and had about eight hundred books, three hundred of which were granted by the Dowager Countess from the school library, which she had started in the village some years previously. Jones[xxiv] mentioned that in the *Parliamentary Educational Blue Book* for the years 1854-5 reference was made to the 'excellent provision which this Institute at Harewood made for the villagers'.

The Great Turnpike Riots of 1753

Up to the time of the riot, Leeds had never been properly connected with good roads to the key centres in the county. The attempt to improve the quality of the roads, and to pay for them by the erection of turnpike bars, was the cause of the riot. Although various historians have a slightly different view of exactly what happened, the following, I believe, is an accurate amalgamation of the various versions.

---

10. Ralph Thoresby (1658-1725) was the first historian of Leeds. In honour of Thoresby, the Leeds local history society was designated the Thoresby Society on the day of its official launch on 10th July 1889. His principal book, *Ducatus Leodiensis,* was published in 1715.
11. John Boulter was the owner of Harewood Castle and Estate until it was sold to Henry Lascelles in 1739.
12. William de Aldeburgh is credited with creating much of Harewood Castle. When he died in 1388 the castle was held jointly by the Ryther and Redmayne (Redman) families, into which his two daughters had married. In 1574, James Ryther and partner William Plompton bought out the Redman family, although Ryther's financial situation must have worsened because he died in London's Fleet Prison in 1595.
13. The building that housed the Institute is now the village chapel. Services are held here every Sunday and alternate between Methodist and Anglican services.

A large body of men from the manufacturing districts of Leeds destroyed the toll bar at Halton Dial (York Road), one at Beeston and one on the Leeds Bradford Road. They then informed Edwin Lascelles that they intended to demolish his toll bar as well. On the afternoon of 25th June 1753 about three hundred men, armed with swords and clubs were seen to be approaching Harewood Bridge from the direction of Weardley. Edwin Lascelles at the head of about eighty of his tenants and workmen (whom he had armed), met them in a field not far from the Harewood Bridge toll bar. After a severe fight in which many on both sides were wounded, a number of insurgents were arrested.[14] The mob became so exasperated at the defeat and capture of some of its members that they threatened to pull down Edwin Lascelles residence, Gawthorpe Hall. However, the arrival of dragoons from York persuaded them that it was wiser to withdraw.

The arrested men were then, according to Davey[xxv] taken before magistrates at Briggate in Leeds the following day and, according to Buckle[xxvi], ten were later committed to York Castle. The proceedings aroused the fury of the mob to a fever pitch and they attempted a rescue of the insurgents. The dragoons from York were in attendance and after reading the Riot Act to no avail, a volley of powder was fired! Unfortunately, this did not have the desired effect, and served only to incense the fury of the mob. The soldiers again fired, this time with 'ball'. The mob suddenly fled in all directions; upwards of thirty people were wounded, several fatally. According to Jones[xxvii] eight were killed and fifty wounded, many of whom died later from their injuries. Thus ended the great turnpike riots of 1753, although the dragoons were stationed at Harewood and Harewood Bridge for some time afterwards.

Extinct Villages[15]

Several hundred years ago Harewood was not the village it is today but a considerable township and market town. Several of the villages within this township have become extinct: Stockton, Lofthouse, Henhouse, Stubhouse, Stank and Gawthorpe. In addition, the following, very much not extinct villages or areas, were originally in the Parish and Manor of Harewood: Alwoodley, Wike, Wigton, Rigton, Weardley, Weeton, Dunkeswick and East Keswick.

---

14.   The number of insurgents arrested was three, according to John Davey, or thirty according to Buckle.

15.   The main reference for this section was taken from the *History and Antiquities of Harewood* by John Jones.

Stockton

This village was mentioned in the Domesday Book. The remains of the village, half a mile East of Harewood, still existed in the 18th Century and the name is still shown on the 2004 Ordnance Survey map. As many querns (a hand-mill for grinding corn) had been found there, historians believe that Stockton was either a station or encampment during the Roman era. Its situation must have been delightful – it stood on the summit of a hill overlooking the valley of the Wharfe in one direction, and in the other the plain of York; while on the North East the Hambledon Hills could be seen. Stockton does not appear in a list of West Riding villages given in the Warburton Collection of the Lansdowne Mss.[16], therefore presumably the village itself was no longer in existence prior to 1600. However, farms currently occupy the site and are still called Stockton.

Lofthouse

This village stood in the park on the left hand side of the Leeds/Harrogate Turnpike road, just below the iron gates. It was a separate manor and was also mentioned in the Domesday Book. Lofthouse is included in the list of villages in the Warburton Collection of the Lansdowne Mss. in connection with a number of neighbouring villages. There were two public houses in Lofthouse and in the old maps the locality is dotted over with cottages.

In the deed of sale, when the Harewood Estate was purchased from the Earl of Strafford by Sir John Cutler, there were a number of tenant farmers named, all holding farms in Lofthouse. As in the case of Stockton, farmhouses remain which show where the village stood and still retain its name. Lofthouse Grange and Lofthouse Farm are both shown on the 2004 Ordnance Survey map.

Henhouse

One village, not mentioned in the Domesday Book, has entirely disap-peared, and its location and name seems to be forgotten. In the research carried out by Jones, he found some evidence in the Dodsworth Mss, vol. 122, fol. 127, that a place called Tonehouse in Harewood existed in about the year 1309. Jewell, in his book, alludes to a village called Henhouse, fixing its position about a quarter of a mile East of the Castle. He believed that it derived its name from the poultry yard of the castle. This, however, Jones imagined to be conjecture on Jewell's part, as there was a large parcel of

---

16.   According to the British Library website, Lansdowne Mss refers to the collection of Manuscripts (Mss) collected by Sir William Petty, 1st Marquess of Lansdowne (1737-1805) and including the papers of William Cecil, Lord Burghley. This collection was purchased by the British Museum in 1807.

land called Hencroft, near the place alluded to. "As it lies a considerable distance from the castle, it cannot be the site of this extinct village, which is expressly stated in the extract from the Mss. to be a part of the park."[xxviii] Tonehouse does not occur in the list of West Riding villages given in the Lansdowne Mss. referred to above.

Stubhouse

Stubhouse, now the same of a solitary farmhouse, South West of Harewood, was formerly a large village and was also mentioned in the Domesday Book, being listed as a manor. Stub House Plantation and Stub House Farm, both North of Eccup Reservoir, can be found on the 2004 Ordnance Survey map.

Stank

This place was anciently called Hetheric, and was both a manor and lordship in Harewood. The name Stank was often used in the North of England in places which had standing waters or pools – probably from Latin 'stagnum' or the French 'estang'. All traces of the village are now gone, although farm buildings and workshops belonging to the Estate are situated there. Part of the Ebor Way around the Harewood Estate passes through the area called Stank and over a bridge near the old fish pond.

Gawthorpe

The exact situation of the village of Gawthorpe is not known. It stood somewhere between the Old Hall and Stank, and its derivation from Isl. gouke, the cuckoo, (the cuckoo's village) shows that its position must have been thoroughly rural. It was a separate village and manor, and is enumerated as such in a list of West Riding towns and villages, in the Lansdowne Mss. As was often the case, it gave the surname to a family, the last representative of which, Maud, daughter and heiress of John de Gawkethorp, married William Gascoigne, in about 1135. By this marriage it became the property and residence of the Gascoignes.

20th and 21st Centuries

Turn of the Century to Post World War I
According to Kennedy,[xxix] Harewood was perhaps slower than many English villages to lose the structure of pre-war society. Villages in other parts of the country lost their young farm workers who found that easier livings could be made in the factories and salesrooms of towns. However, it seems that after the war the men were happy to return to their community in the rich agricultural land of Wharfedale, at least for a while.

Harewood, like many rural communities, escaped the bombings suffered by larger towns and cities, but there were other effects including, of course, the loss of the men who did not return from war. War horses were stabled behind the Harewood Arms whilst resting from front-line duty and the village blacksmith[17] often had to work through the night. In 1915, Harewood House was turned into a hospital for officers (the same happened in World War II). Lord Harewood was also President of the West Riding Territorial Association.

For those who did return from the war, life would be changed forever. Most of the men had seen nothing of life outside Wharfedale before joining the army. After their experiences, the excitement of a trip to Leeds, and time spent either in the village pub or on the cricket pitch, were not as enticing as they once were.

Another contributor to the changes to village life was brought about by taxation. As Kennedy pointed out,

> "Lloyd George[18], who doubtless still ranks high in the demonology of England's remaining landowners, has generally been blamed as the first to destroy village life by introducing the taxation which effectively broke up the great estates. What he began, of course, was completed by the social upheaval of two world wars, the flight from the land into industry and the inexorable intermingling of urban and country ways by the car, telephone, radio, television (*and now the internet*). It is undoubtedly the presence of a historic house and working estate, however truncated, that has enabled Harewood village and others like it to retain much of their original character. Without them, a village in such close proximity to industrial cities would long since have been swallowed up in the kind of 'creeping' suburbia that began to disfigure the countryside in the 1920s."[xxx]

---

17.   Over time the village blacksmith shop became the village petrol station but now is a vacant site on the left hand side of the Leeds/Harrogate Road.
18.   David Lloyd George was born in Manchester but grew up in Wales and became a Welsh-speaking Welshman, the only Welshman ever to hold the office of Prime Minister in the British Government. Although he was Prime Minister from 7 December 1916 to 22 October 1922, it was when he was Chancellor of the Exchequer in the Asquith Government in 1909 that he introduced his famous 'People's Budget'. He introduced his so called 'supertax' on those earning over £5000 per year, an increase in death duties on the estates of the rich and heavy taxes on profits gained from the ownership and sale of property. Basically, he strongly believed in re-distribution of wealth.

The 1920s to 1940s

In the early 1920s, horses were still the main form of transportation, apart from walking of course, and the roads were so quiet that this is where children used to play marbles and other games. Horse-drawn carts used to pull into the yard in front of the Harewood Arms, whose entrepreneurial landlord used to operate his own charabanc service to the outskirts of Leeds. It took the best part of an hour to make the four mile journey from Harewood to Moortown where you could get a tram into Leeds. Kennedy[xxxi] pointed out that you could see a show at the City Varieties (the setting for BBC Television's 'Good Old Days' music-hall programme), pay for your fish and chip dinner and tram fare, and still have change from a shilling!

During the period between the wars, the Harewood Estate was ever present in the lives of the villagers. Employment came either from the farms in the area, or the Harewood Estate which would have required labourers, gamekeepers, grooms, forestry workers, chauffeurs and domestic servants. For many, life revolved around the arrival of important guests and the logistics of moving the Lascelles family between Harewood and London.

The 1950s and 1960s

A number of Council houses were built in the late 1950s – these were architecturally rather special ones; built of local stone from demolished old cottages, designed to blend in with Carr's 18th Century terraces.

The Village Hall on Church Lane was opened by HRH The Princess Royal and the Countess of Harewood on 6th September 1959. One of the reasons for building the new Village Hall was to replace the Institute. As often happens, the new Hall was proposed many years before it was finally built! In actual fact, virtually every issue of the *Harewood News* throughout the 1930s featured at least one article pertaining to the proposed Village Hall. Furthermore, for a very long time, the plan was for the Village Hall to be built on the East side of Harrogate Road, not on Church Lane. The main headline in the April 1939 issue of the *Harewood News* was 'Harewood Village Hall Plans go Through!' The first paragraph of the article was,

> "We have pleasure in announcing that the negotiations between the Village Hall Committee, the Architect, the National Fitness Council and the National Council for Social Services have resulted in a provisional grant from the National Fitness Council of £1500, and a grant of £500 from the National Council for Social Services. Such a splendid result compensates for the delay which

has been necessary to produce a scheme which would meet with the approval of the various Councils concerned and we are sure that any disappointment our readers may have felt at the delay on commencing building operations will now turn to congratulations on the splendid result achieved."

Many fundraising activities took place in order to raise money for the new Village Hall – for example, articles of clothing were made that were then sold at events at Harewood House and various whist drives were held. Also, Harewood House was specially opened on at least one Bank Holiday. According to a number of villagers, Appleyards of Leeds gave a mini to be raffled off and the money went towards the building of the Village Hall.

The Hall was eventually built on a plot of land owned by the Earl of Harewood and using stone from old farm buildings. Although the exterior must have been attractive when it was first built, it has been left to decay for many, many years and now is more of an eyesore than anything. In fact, on his first tour of the village, a recent village bobby was convinced that the building was, in fact, derelict!

In 1961 the historic old toll bar house at Harewood Bridge which had been the scene of the 1753 turnpike riot was pulled down by Wetherby Rural District Council as unsafe.

The 1970s and 1980s
Harewood village changed significantly in the period between the 1970s and the 1980s. Harewood was not alone, as this was happening to villages all over the country. The trend that began in the 1970s – a smaller and smaller number of people working directly or indirectly for the Harewood Estate – continues today. Both commuters and retirees from the more affluent parts of Leeds were moving into the village.

Around 1970, further houses were built on Church Lane, initially intended for use by a Police Unit, with a detached Sergeant's house and two semi-detached houses for the Constables. They are still referred to as the 'police houses' by villagers.

Lord Harewood sold three acres of land which adjoined the park and the Estate office to a Leeds developer in 1976, but insisted that the new development had to be personally approved by him. The Harewood Mews was built on this land and do not look out of place within their 18th Century surroundings. However, Kennedy quoted someone who said that "in the old days people had no money but they had heart in their bellies. Now they have money but no heart" and "If they'd put cows or horses on the three acres it would have done more good for the village".[xxxii] I am quite certain that the residents of The Mews would still be rather upset by these comments!

Harewood was changing significantly in terms of the on-going transition from a traditional village with a variety of local shops and a 'village feel' to that of a 'dormitory' for those who are still working, or a delightful rural retreat for those who have retired. The Square, for instance, once the heart of the village, is now empty of businesses, except for the GP Surgery.

With the local government reorganisation of 1974, Harewood's connections with the Rural District Council of Wetherby were severed and it became part of Leeds Metropolitan District Council.

In the late 1970s, the land of Castle Farm was sold to property developers and five large houses were built in the early 1980s.

Although the above refers to many changes that took place in the village in the 1970s and the 1980s, one event has thus far remained unmentioned, the opening of the Sports and Social Club at the back of the Village Hall. This followed a temporary closure of the Harewood Arms in 1970 because the licensee forgot to renew the licence! The first pint served in the Sports and Social Club was to one Walter Wild, father of Olive Wild, on 3 June 1970. A framed picture of a very proud Walter Wild hung in Olive Wild's house for many years.

The 1990s up to 2007
In many ways the 1990s through to the current day has marked a time of stagnation and decline for Harewood village. Yes, the village itself, and its magnificent views, has remained unaltered but virtually nothing new has been added. During this time there were no new houses built within the village, the petrol station (the former blacksmiths) was pulled down and is now an empty space waiting for something to be done with it, the Village Hall continues to decline in both usage and state of repair and a number of former clubs or activities have either disappeared altogether or changed their venue. For example, the Harewood WI, one of the first in the country established in 1919, was finally disbanded in 2005. The Friendship Club continues to meet in the Village Hall on the first Tuesday of each month but I would not want to speculate as to how much longer this will continue meeting in the Village Hall. The village Supper Club used to meet monthly

in the Village Hall but has moved to the Harewood Arms because of the poor state of repair of the Village Hall.

Throughout this period many of the houses owned by the Harewood Estate have been sold and the number of people living in the village who work directly for the Estate continues to decline. With many newcomers buying houses in the village and with fewer direct links with the Estate, the village could be described as being more like a dormitory for those who work in Leeds or Harrogate. For many villages there is a focal point in which people can come together in order for the 'locals' to continue their on-going relationships and for 'newcomers' to meet the locals. The Harewood Arms serves as the main focal point today. The Village Hall and the Sports and Social Club might have served that purpose in the past but that does not seem to be the case any longer. Yes, many of the old faces who have been going to the Sports and Social Club since it opened in 1970 are still spending time and money there, as are their descendents, but few newcomers use the Club.

However, at the time of writing in the Spring of 2007, a bit of entrepreneurial flair seems to be emerging from the Village Hall. Each Sunday a sign stating 'Village Hall Tea Room' is placed in front of the Hall, a menu is hung on the wall and the Village Hall is ready to do business as a tea room. I certainly hope they are successful and that some of the money raised will be ploughed back in to the fabric of the dilapidated building.

Harewood's Chapel, which is joint Methodist and Anglican, could also serve the purpose of being a focal point for the village. Unfortunately, there are only a small number of residents who attend services regularly although numbers do increase on special occasions – Christmas, Easter, Harvest Festival and so on. Being part of the congregation does encourage a sense of community and fellowship and my wife and I have made many friends through both Harewood's Chapel and St Oswald's Church in Collingham.

I suspect that you may find all of this a bit gloomy and that you will have heard very similar stories before. In other words, a village making the transition to feeling more like a dormitory is, unfortunately, becoming very common place throughout England. Having said all of that, does it mean that Harewood village is not a pleasant place in which to live? Not at all! It is most certainly a very desirable place in which to live and when houses come up for sale, which is not all that often, they are both very expensive and don't stay unsold for very long. So what makes it so desirable? The answer: location, location, location. Location in terms of convenience for Leeds, Harrogate and even York. Location in terms of escaping from the rat race of town or city living. And, of course, location in terms of the wonderful countryside. Also, it is worth pointing out that the residents are friendly but would certainly not be described as 'in-your-face'. In other words, people are generally very approachable and friendly but if you want to be left alone, that is ok with them too. In addition, I am sure that those who have lived in Harewood for a long time – perhaps all their lives – will feel a much stronger sense of community than those who are more recent arrivals. It is a beautiful place to live but as in any area, it is up to the residents to make an effort to create a community rather than simply a place in which to live. It is important to remember that shops, village halls and pubs, no matter how lovely or plentiful they might, or might not be, do not make communities – people do.

Whilst it is true that little has changed in terms of the infrastructure of the village itself, much has changed in the Harewood area. Here are some examples. In 1997 Emmerdale[19] Village was built on the Harewood Estate and that in itself has brought Emmerdale 'tourists' to the village. In other words, people come to Harewood to see the area in which the television series is filmed. Whilst walkers are not allowed to visit Emmerdale Village itself, except on guided/organised tours, they can certainly see the roof tops of the village whilst walking around the Harewood Estate. Harewood Village Hall has been used for many years as a type of 'staging post' for the Emmerdale film crews and actors when they are filming outside shots within the woods and Harewood generally.

In 2003 sheep grazing in the area just beyond the cattle grid along the bridle way leaving Harewood via Church Lane were replaced by red and roe deer. The herds are thriving and give much pleasure to both the locals and tourists alike. In a similar vane, the red kite population that began with only a few breeding pairs when they were introduced to the Estate in the late 1990s, has been a total success. It is not uncommon to see six to ten, or sometimes even more, red kites soaring overhead every single day.

As you will see in Chapter Four, Harewood Castle underwent a massive conservation project in 2004/2005 in order to stabilise the ruins and, perhaps, ultimately to allow limited access to the Castle area by tourists.

Throughout the 1990s and into the 2000s the Harewood Estate and the Harewood 'experience' has changed and developed each year. Harewood House and Estate are now one of Yorkshire's major tourist attractions.

---

19.   Emmerdale is a TV 'soap opera' filmed by Yorkshire Television.

Finally, let us not forget that Broadband came to Harewood in the Spring of 2004!

End Notes

i   John Jones, *The History and Antiquities of Harewood* (1859), p 9.
ii   Harewood – *Topographical Dictionary of Yorkshire* (1822), Information from GenUK, p 1.
iii   John Jewell, *The Tourist's Companion of the History and Antiquities of Harewood* (1819), p 3.
iv   Ron Wade, *Vat Sal Be Sal* (1982), p 7.
v   A H Smith (1961) as referenced in E Dennison and S Richardson, *Harewood Castle, Harewood, West Yorkshire: An Archaeological and Architectural Condition Survey* (forthcoming), p 1.
vi   Wade, op cit, p 7.
vii   Harewood House Trust, *Harewood: A Guide*, p 4.
viii   Carol Kennedy, *Harewood: The Life and Times of an English Country House* (1982), p 22.
ix   Jones, op cit, p 165.
x   E Dennison and S Richardson, *Harewood Castle, Harewood, West Yorkshire: An Archaeological and Architectural Condition Survey* (unpublished EDAS report for Harewood Estate), (forthcoming), p 1.
xi   W H Buckle, *A Guide for the Information of Schools* (1975), p 19.
xii   Jones, op cit, p 166.
xiii   Wade, op cit, p 42
xiv   Buckle, op cit. p 19.
xv   Ibid, p 19.
xvi   Kennedy, op cit, p 69.
xvii   Jewell, op cit, p 3.
xviii James Walvin, *The Colonial Origins of English Wealth: The Harewoods of Yorkshire* (unpublished paper, 2003), p 7.
xix   Joseph Ismay, *A Visit to Chapel Allerton and Harewood in 1767*, Transcribed by E Kitson Clark, annotated by G E Kirk and James B Place (1945), p 339.
xx   Ethel Wade, *Wesleyan-Methodist Chapels* (2006), p 7.
xxi   Buckle, op cit, p 20.
xxii   Kennedy, op cit, p 70.
xxiii Buckle, op cit, p 20.
xxiv   Jones, op cit, pp 179 and 180.
xxv   John Davey, *A Couple of Tours of Elmet*, A Ch4 Time Team Programme (1997), p 1. (Downloaded from the Internet on 2nd March 2006)
xxvi   Buckle, op cit, p 20.
xxvii Jones, op cit, p169.
xxviii Ibid, p 197.
xxix   Kennedy, op cit, p 109.
xxx   Ibid, pp 169-170.
xxxi   Ibid, p 111.
xxxii Ibid, p 169.

CHAPTER THREE
Harewood Church – All Saints

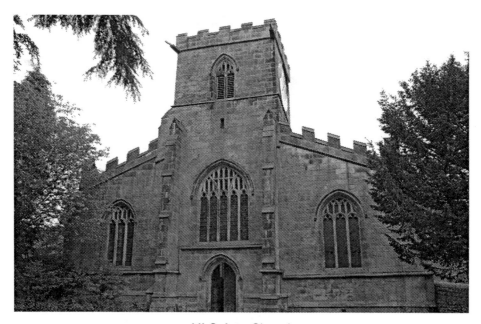

All Saints Church

Introduction

> *Draw close to Harewood Church, the Church of All Saints,*
> *Serenely standing through the turbulent centuries.*
> *Now peaceful, silent with her Lords and Ladies.*
> *Here rest Harewood people beneath Harewood skies,*
> *Winter grass, and the purity and promise of January snowdrops.*
> Iaian Wade[i]

All Saints Church, or Harewood Church, stands within the grounds of the Harewood House Estate and is half a mile West of the village of Harewood. The Church is classified as being in the 'northern Perpendicular architectural style', also known as the last phase of English Gothic style, which dated from the late 14th Century to the middle of the 16th Century.

As I could find no finer words to describe the Church than those of Edmund Bogg[ii] I will paraphrase his description. All Saints Church is a venerable structure embowered on all sides by woodland; seen from the park, it forms a picture whose charm of contrast and holy sweetness would require the pencil of a Claude and the pen of a Ruskin to delineate. Graceful beeches and stately chestnuts provide shade and coolness across the woodland path, where joyous birds hide under greenwood shade, sing merry notes on every branch and bough; whilst the tower, under a circle of sweeping trees cannot fail to impress the beholder with the beauty and loveliness of its surroundings.

Although Bogg wrote these words more than a hundred years ago, I could not find anything that does not still apply to the Church today. It is wonderful when some things never change. Having said that, although the description of the outside of the Church has not changed much over the years, there have been considerable changes made to the inside of the Church, and what has happened to the Church itself over the centuries is a fascinating story in its own right.

All Saints Church over the Centuries

A number of historians have stated that there was some sort of Church on, or near this site, from about 830 AD. According to Griffith,[iii] there was a diligent and saintly priest by the name of Farmon who was a devoted disciple of Macregal, a Scribe-Bishop of Birr in Ireland. Macregal and Farmon worked together on the translation of the Gospels. When the Norsemen came they killed Bishop Macregal and plundered his house. Farmon escaped with the precious manuscript and is said to have settled in the forest of Harewood where he built a wattle Church and ministered to the people of the hamlet. One of Farmon's major achievements is that he translated the Gospel of St Matthew which is now in the Bodleian Library at Oxford.

Between 830 AD and when All Saints Church was founded in the 12th Century, no factual information could be found. However, you could specu-late that there was at least some historic link between St Oswald's Church in Collingham and that which became All Saints Church. There are a number of reasons for this speculation. Firstly, Collingham is less than five miles from Harewood and given that Harewood was better known and much larger than Collingham between the 9th and 12th Centuries, I believe that people, including priests, would have travelled between the two places. Secondly, in

St Oswald's Church there are substantial fragments of two Anglo-Saxon crosses (also known as Collingham Crosses) – the Apostle's Cross dated between the 8th and 10th Centuries and a second Runic Cross decorated with intertwined dragons, thought to date from the 9th Century. Much of the stonework of the nave and chancel are thought to be Saxon and thus predate the Norman Conquest of 1066. Given that both Harewood and Collingham therefore have histories that predate the Norman Conquest and since there was evidence of Christianity in Harewood, yet no evidence of a Church between 830 AD and the building of All Saints Church in the 12th Century, I believe that it is easy to speculate that Collingham could have been the focal point for Christians living in or near Harewood. Strangely enough, although Harewood was mentioned in the Domesday Book, Collingham was not.

What is certain is that William de Curci (or Curcy) founded the Church in Harewood in 1116 and it was originally dedicated to the Holy Cross. During the restoration of 1793 a Latin inscription was found carved on an old beam, which was translated as: "we adore and praise Thee, thou holy Jesus, because Thou hast redeemed us by The Holy Cross" and dated 1116.

Of the original Church, nearly all traces have disappeared, apart from a fine Norman font with its cable moulding. Before offering more information about the Holy Cross, I will digress to clarify a story which has been told about William de Curci's son. Acccording to sources, including Griffith[iv], "the son of William and Avicia, Romelli, was drowned in the River Wharfe whilst out hunting in Barden Woods. In his memory, his mother founded the Priory of Bolton, now one of the most beautiful ruins in Yorkshire. The story of the drowned son has been immortalised by Wordsworth in his touching little poem:

> Young Romelli through Barden Woods
> Is ranging high and low
> And holds a greyhound in a leash
> To let slip upon buck or doe."

Further research, however, shows that this story actually relates to the death of William's nephew, not his son, and it was Alice of Skipton Castle rather than her sister Avicia of Harewood, who gave land to the Augustinian Canons on which they subsequently built Bolton Priory. It seems that Harewood was also linked to Bolton Abbey/Priory as it is said that Avicia gave the income from flax mills at Harewood, amounting to £12 annually, for the upkeep of the Abbey and perhaps this is why the Church of Harewood was served by the monks of Bolton.

In relation to the short poem mentioned above, I suspect that many of you will have a number of questions. For example, is that the whole poem, did Wordsworth actually visit Yorkshire, and so on. The extract above is but a very small piece from a poem entitled *The Force of Prayer* or *The Founding of Bolton Priory* that Wordsworth wrote in 1807, around the same time that he wrote his long narrative poem *The White Doe of Rylstone*. It seems that Wordsworth was inspired by history, landscape, popular legend, and a ballad entitled *The Rising of the North*[1]. I was able to discover that Wordsworth visited the area around Bolton Priory in the Summer of 1807 and that the first half of the poem was composed at Stockton-upon-Tees when he and his wife were visiting her eldest brother, near the end of the year. He continued to work on it when he returned to Grasmere and it was sent to his publisher in 1808. It would appear that the area in which the accident took place is a cleft in the rocks, through which the Wharfe runs, called 'The Strid'.

Although the above excerpt was all that Griffith included in his writing, I feel that you might enjoy a longer extract from the poem, which will help you to understand more clearly what happened to the young boy.

> *Young Romelli through Barden Woods*
> *Is raging high and low;*
> *And holds a greyhound in a leash,*
> *To let slip upon buck or doe.*
>
> *The pair have reached that fearful chasm,*
> *How tempting to bestride!*
> *For lordly Wharf is there pent in*
> *With rocks on either side.*
>
> *This striding place is called THE STRID,*
> *A name which it took of yore:*
> *A thousand years hath it borne that name,*
> *And shall a thousand more.*
>
> *And hither is young Romelli come,*
> *And what may now forbid*
> *That he, perhaps for the hundredth time,*
> *Shall bound across "The Strid"?*

---

1.   The Rising of the North was led by two Catholic nobleman from the North, Charles Neville, 6th Earl of Westmorland and Thomas Percy, 7th Earl of Northumberland, against Elizabeth I in 1569.

He sprang in glee – for what cared he
That the river was strong, and the rocks were steep!
But the greyhound in the leash hung back,
And checked him in his leap.

The boy is in the arms of Wharf,
And strangled by a merciless force;
For never more was young Romelli seen
Till he rose a lifeless corpse.

Now there is stillness in the vale,
And long unspeaking sorrow:
Wharf shall be, to pitying hearts,
A name more sad than Yarrow.

If for a lover the lady wept,
A solace she might borrow
From death, and from the passion of death
Old Wharf might heal her sorrow.

Long, long in darkness did she sit,
And her first words were, "Let there be
In Bolton, on the field of Wharf,
A stately priory!"

Back to a brief history of the Holy Cross. In olden times the Holy Cross was known as Holy Rood or Old Holy Rood. According to Jewell,[v] the inhabitants of Harewood held an annual Feast which was the first Sunday after Old Holy Rood. The Feast of the Holy Cross or Holy Rood is 14th September.

There was a short piece in the *Harewood News* of September 1938[vi] about the Harewood Feast. According to this, in 312 AD, the Roman General Constantine was leading his army towards Rome to fight a battle which would ultimately make him Emperor. The army of the enemy was much larger than his own and Constantine must have felt some trepidation as the battle drew near. As he was marching through the Swiss mountains, he saw a vision in the sky – a cross of light with the words, 'In this sign conquer' beneath. Constantine was so impressed that he ordered a cross-bar to be fixed to a spear to form a cross and this was carried instead of the usual bronze eagle as the standard at the head of his army. On the banks of the Tiber he met and defeated his rival and in gratitude he made the cross the banner of his legions. In the Calendar of the Church, 14th September is Holy Cross Day, a festival to commemorate Constantine's victory.

Further research into the history of the Holy Cross has revealed a different version of events, which is in about the same timeframe and still linked to Constantine. According to this, the event is believed to celebrate the day in 326 AD when it is said that St Helena found the True Cross (the cross of Christ) in the Holy Lands. St Helena was 80 when she and a few colleagues searched for, and found, three crosses. It was suggested by St Macarius of Jerusalem that she took the three crosses to a woman afflicted with an incurable disease and had her touch each one. One of them immediately cured her and it was pronounced the True Cross. She built a church on the spot where the cross was found and sent pieces to Rome and Constantinople.

As the writer in the *Harewood News* pointed out, originally the Feast was more religious and people gave thanks for their Church, but as time moved on, it became more social and secular. As of today, people tend to remember it as simply a Feast or Festival, but do not remember the origins of the event.

Harewood's Church of the Holy Cross was re-dedicated as All Saints in the 13th Century. No evidence has been found as to why the name was changed.

In the time of Edward II (1307-27), the Scots penetrated into this part of Yorkshire, leaving ruin and devastation behind. During the raids, the Churches of Harewood and Adel were greatly damaged. However, nothing has been found to say if anything happened during this raid to St Oswald's Church in Collingham. Perhaps at this time St Oswald's was in a poor state of repairs and thus the Scots thought it was not worth the effort to destroy it further. Alternatively perhaps the Scots simply overlooked it. Who knows? Although it was not recorded just how badly the Church in Harewood was damaged, it was, according to Kennedy[vii] completely rebuilt in the reign of Edward III (1327-77) and underwent further extensive alteration in the 15th Century. According to David Hey[viii], the rebuilding of the Church was completed in 1424 and was paid for by Bolton Priory. Hence the reason why so many historians make reference to All Saints Church being a fine example of a 15th Century Church.

In the later Middle Ages (1400 to 1500), rather than giving to monasteries, wealthy people often sought to improve their own Parish Church or to attach a private chantry[2] chapel to an aisle or chancel. The majority of Yorkshire chantries recorded at the Dissolution, were founded after the

---

2.   A chantry is a mini-chapel originally intended as a place where prayers would be said for the soul of the rich person who had paid for it. Chantry is a term for the English establishment of a shrine or chapel on private land where monks or priests would say (or 'chant') prayers on a fixed schedule, usually for someone who had died.

Black Death[3]. All Saints Church in Harewood is an example of such patronage.

One of the most significant things about All Saints Church is its collection of six pairs of finely carved and splendidly preserved alabaster effigies and tombs, one of the largest and finest collections in a Parish Church in the country. One of the oldest of the effigies goes back to the early 15th Century and commemorates Judge Gascoigne. Lord Chief Justice, Sir William Gascoigne, who died in 1419[4], 4 years after Agincourt, is, according to Mauchline[ix] "known chiefly for his dignified and apocryphal appearance in Shakespeare's Henry IV as the judge who committed the future Henry V to prison" for contempt of court, and who would have no part in signing the death warrant of Archbishop Scrope. According to Maidstone[x], Richard Scrope was the Archbishop of York. In a room in the Archbishop's own manor, Bishopthorpe, King Henry IV ordered William Gascoigne to pronounce the death sentence against the Archbishop as a traitor to the King. Gascoigne refused by saying, "according to the laws of the kingdom, neither you, my Lord King, nor any of your subjects acting in your name, can legally condemn any bishop to death". The King exploded in a furious rage against the Judge and at once ordered Sir William Fulthorp, a Knight but not a Judge, to pronounce the death sentence on the Archbishop. Archbishop Richard Scrope was sentenced to death, by Sir William Fulthorp, and executed on 8th June 1405 just outside the walls of York.

Without doubt All Saints Church is grand place to visit and to spend time in. Whilst there you might like to look out for the following in particular. First of all, the six alabaster tombs or monuments – all of which are on the right hand side of the church and all contain information on a nearby wall about the people to whom the tombs/monuments are dedicated.

(I)   Sir William Gascoigne – Chief Justice – who died in 1419 and his wife Elizabeth Mowbray – daughter and co-heiress of Sir William Mowbray of Kirklington. No date is shown for her death.

---

3.   The Black Death is the name given to a disease called the bubonic plague which was rampant during the 14th Century. In Medieval England, the Black Death was to kill 1.5 million people out of an estimated total population of 4 million between 1348 and 1350. No medical knowledge existed in Medieval England to cope with the disease. After 1350, it was to strike England another six times before the end of the Century. The Black Death was caused by fleas carried by rats that were very common in towns and cities. The fleas bit into their victims literally injecting them with the disease. Death could be very quick for the weaker victims. Its symptoms were described in 1348 by a man called Boccaccio who lived in Florence, Italy.

4.   Although Mauchline (1992, 16) stated that Sir William Gascoigne died in 1429, all other sources of information gave the date of his death as 1419.

(II)   Sir Richard Redman who died in 1426 and his wife Elizabeth Aldburgh – daughter of Sir William Aldburgh and co-heiress of Harewood Castle – who died in 1434.

(III) Sir William Ryther who died in 1426 and his wife Sybil Aldburgh – co-heiress with her sister Elizabeth of Harewood Castle – who died in 1440.

(IV)   Sir William Gascoigne - Grandson of Judge Gascoigne (I) – who died in 1465 and his wife Margaret Clarwell. No date is shown for her death.

(V)   Sir William Gascoigne - Grandson of Sir William Gascoigne (IV) who died in 1487 and his wife Margaret Percy. No date is shown for her death.

(VI)   Edward Redman – Great Grandson of Sir Richard Redman (II) – who died in 1510 and his wife Elizabeth Huddlestone who died in 1529.

The final thing that should be mentioned about the tombs or monuments is that they represent a very valuable record of the costumes, the armour and the art of carving in alabaster in the 15th and early 16th Centuries.

Other items of special interest are the Norman font as mentioned earlier, the Sanctuary rail which was given by HRH The Princess Mary (Princess Royal) as a memorial to her father, King George V (1865-1936)[5], and a fragment of a cross shaft thought to be an Anglo-Scandinavian sculpture from the Viking Period (10th and early 11th Century). This was discovered in 1981 during the conservation of the Ryther-Aldburgh alabaster monument (III). As with the tombs/monuments, information about these can be found on the walls in the Church.

Although no historian has explained why it happened, when Edwin Lascelles was occupied in intensifying the medieval aspect of All Saints, the stained glass of the period was lost and only a few fragments have been recovered. Moreover, the medieval furnishings – the stalls for the priests, the seats and the screens of oak – were taken out in what one mid-19th

---

5.   According to an article in the *Harewood News* of August 1938, the Archbishop of Canterbury dedicated the new altar rails and the service was conducted by the Rev M G Lascelles (one of the Earl's relatives) and Rev H H Griffith. The article ended by stating that the Archbishop spent the weekend at Harewood House.

Century historian, John Jones, called 'a series of the most barbarous alterations'.

You might be interested to know that the stone for both Harewood Castle and All Saints Church came from the Harewood estate quarry. Mauchline[xi] made the point that "geologically it was part of the Yorkshire Millstone Grit series and is composed of Upper Follifoot Gritstone, an extremely fine and durable stone".

Mauchline[xii] said that Old Gawthorpe Hall had a fine chapel, but "Edwin Lascelles can never have considered it adequate" and that "there were some abortive plans for a chapel in Harewood House, one by Adam and another by Carr, but All Saints became the family's place of worship and burial." She went on to say that, "from the first, Lascelles apparently viewed the church as a romantic gothic eye-catcher. In 1759, the year in which the building of the house began, Robert Adam made drawings 'to add finishing to the top of the steeple in the Gothick taste'." However, "this remained unexecuted and it was not until 1793 that Lascelles had the east elevation decorated with gothic battlements, pinnacles and window tracery".

When Edwin Lascelles died in 1795, five years after being ennobled, a family vault was constructed under the Church. Since then, generation after generation of Lascelles have been buried in this family vault, the last being HRH The Princess Royal in 1965.

I found Mauchline's description of the route visitors take to Harewood House via the view of All Saints Church to be fascinating.

> "It is significant that the avenue to the house was aligned so that visitors could appreciate first of all the markedly 'Gothick' character of the east end of the church, before the path curved away to the left to bring them within sight of the impressive, classical entrance front of the new house. It was the subtle and effective contrast, a manipulation of landscape to suggest ancient lineage and fashionable good taste, the fruit of wealth and success."[xiii]

Mauchline[xiv] mentioned that the first Lord Lascelles loved music. "He had his own band of musicians and, as a local patron, saw to it that Harewood Church produced a reasonably well-trained choir. The organist, John White, was retained almost as a member of the household. As early as April 1795, his expenses were paid to London; thereafter, regular fees for his services occurred in Lord Harewood's account book." The love of music clearly passed down through the family line of Lascelles but especially to the current Lord Harewood who is very committed to music and the performing arts and is a world-renowned expert, especially in opera.

In 1862-63 All Saints was to undergo yet more restoration, this time at the hand of Sir George Gilbert Scott, who was the architect of St Pancras Station and the Albert Memorial. During this restoration the old glass was replaced, a wooden roof substituted for the 18th Century plasterwork and a new altar, font, pulpit and lectern provided.

It is remarkable that over a period of more than 600 years, there were only 32 vicars of All Saints from Father Laur de Wath (although Edmund Bogg gave the name and title as Canon Laurence de Wath) in 1354 to H H Griffith, the incumbent from 1928 to 1974.

The Church continued to flourish until the late 1960s when it is said that some of the congregation became less willing to walk the half mile from the village!

All Saints Becomes Redundant

Following the sudden death of Rev Griffith in July 1974, the future of Harewood Church was uncertain. However, services continued to be held there, usually led by Rev John Scott, Vicar of Collingham, until All Saints was officially declared redundant in January 1977. From the end of that month, services in Harewood were held in the Methodist Chapel on The Avenue (which became the combined Anglican-Methodist Chapel and is still used today). St Oswald's Church in Collingham became the Parish Church for the new Parish of Collingham with Harewood.

According to Routh and Knowles[xv], there was then some doubt over the future fate of the fabric of the Church. Representations were made to the Church Commissioners both for and against the Church being vested in the Redundant Churches Fund (now known as the Churches Conservation Trust). A number of schemes were suggested and local press reported that the Queen would be consulted about the proposals.

The Church Commissioners finally decided that All Saints should indeed be vested in the Redundant Churches Fund (Churches Conservation Trust) and this was completed in October 1978. The following entry appeared in their Annual Report for 1978:

The large 15th Century church near Leeds has a superb setting in the park of Harewood House. It is now some distance away from the village, which was rebuilt in its present position by Edwin Lascelles in the 18th Century. Apart from some Gothick embellishments to east and west ends in 1793, the church is entirely in the Yorkshire Perpendicular style[6]. In 1862-63 there was a thorough restoration under Sir George Gilbert Scott which included the renewal of all roofs. The furnishings and stained glass all date from this time or later and are of varying merit and interest. The outstanding feature of Harewood church is the series of six alabaster monuments. Indeed this is the largest, and one of the finest collections of alabaster tombs in the country; but damp is causing some of the tombs to deteriorate and their conservation will be the Fund's chief and most exacting task. Substantial repairs to the building itself are also needed, and steps have already been taken to keep it weathertight and to improve ventilation.

Wade[xvi] said that after the closure of All Saints,

"the Redundant Church Users Committee soon commenced the task of repairs and alterations, the organ being dismantled and refitted in St Anne's Roman Catholic Church at Keighley. By January 1981, beside other renovations, the alabaster tombs were receiving excellent attention; in little over a year they were re-sited after thorough cleaning, revealing they had been originally painted – perhaps all the figures excepting the faces."

All Saints Today

In 1981, All Saints Church was once again open to the public.

Since the time that All Saints became 'redundant' as an active Church, the Redundant Churches Fund (Churches Conservation Trust) has allowed only a very small number of services to take place in the Church each year but other events, such as concerts, are also allowed to take place. Special permission has been granted at times for weddings and christenings.

---

6.   The Perpendicular style is also known as the last phase of the English Gothic. This was a native development that made no concessions to the Italian Renaissance and which inspired church builders for two hundred years until the Reformation brought such activities to an end. (*Yorkshire from AD 1000*)

Although All Saints Church is extremely well known it is also, strangely enough, a well-guarded secret. Access to the Church is only permitted via the grounds of the Harewood House Estate and whilst visitors to the House receive free access to the Church, I suspect that very few visitors walk to it, especially in inclement weather. In the countless visits I have made to the Church, it was virtually empty each time. More people do, of course, visit the Church when classical concerts are held there a few times during the year and, once a year, at the carol service on Christmas Eve, there is standing room only.

On the other hand, the lovely churchyard is visited quite extensively by locals from the village (but again not very often by visitors to the House). Part of the reason why the churchyard remains so pleasant and tranquil is that the Church has a very active churchyard conservation group. Throughout the year, but especially from February to May, the churchyard is awash with colour – snowdrops, then daffodils and finally with bluebells. When the flowering season has finished, the churchyard plays host to the Harewood 'lawnmowers' – small, indigenous black sheep! Another reason why the churchyard remains relatively unvisited is that many Emmerdale 'tourists' and walkers strolling along Church Lane are probably not aware that the churchyard even exists, as there are no signs from the lane up the dirt track to the churchyard.

Whilst worship no longer takes place at All Saints and although it is not the centre of village life as it once was, All Saints Church is still loved by both locals and visitors alike.

End Notes

i   Ron Wade, *Vat Sal Be Sal* (1982), p 57.
ii   Edmund Bogg, *Lower Wharfeland* (1904), p 376.
iii   H H Griffith, *The Story of Harewood and its Church* (extracts from) (no date or page numbers)
iv   Ibid.
v   John Jewell, *The Tourist's Companion of the History and Antiquities of Harewood* (1819), p 15.
vi   Harewood House, *Harewood News*, September 1938.
vii   Carol Kennedy, *Harewood: The Life and Times of an English Country House* (1982), p 27.
viii   David Hey, *Yorkshire from AD 1000* (1986), p 105.
ix   Mary Mauchline, *Harewood House* (1992), p 16.
x   Clement Maidstone, *The Martyrdom of Archbishop Richard Scrope*, Translated with Notes and Commentary by Stephen K Wright (1997). Downloaded from The Catholic University of America website, 17 May 2006, p 2.
xi   Mauchline, op cit, p 18.
xii   Ibid, pp 15 and 16.
xiii   Ibid p 18.
xiv   Ibid, p 112.
xv   Routh and Knowles, *The Medieval Monuments of Harewood* (1983), p 61.
xvi   Wade, op cit, p 56.

CHAPTER FOUR
Harewood Castle

Part of the castle ruins with views across the Wharfe Valley beyond

Introduction

> "Yet, though they halls are silent, though they bowers
> Re-echo back the traveller's lonely tread,
> Again imagination bids thee rise
> In all they dread magnificence and strength;
> Thy drawbridge, fosse, and frowning battlements,
> Portcullis, barbican, and dungeon tower."

The above words were written about Harewood Castle and were found in the book *Lower Wharfeland* by Edmund Bogg (1904)[i].

Although Harewood Castle today is now little more than an extremely impressive ruin on the top of Harewood Bank, it has, over many centuries, had a major impact on Harewood and the surrounding area. The Castle was a ruin when J M W Turner painted it from both a Southerly and a Northerly perspective in c. 1798. The Turner painting from the Southerly perspective gives a far more impressive feel for just how dominant the Castle's position was and why it was built there in the first place. Since the time of Turner the trees have grown and until recently the ivy virtually obliterated sight of the Castle. It is interesting to note that some people believe that the ivy may have been deliberately planted to create a sort of romantic ruin. During the major conservation and stabilisation project that took place in 2004/2005, the ivy was cut back around the shell of the Castle and now motorists travelling on the A61 from Harrogate to Harewood can once again see the remains of the Castle standing proud at the top of Harewood Bank. Now, let us go back in history and find out more about this fascinating building.

When researching for this book I really wanted to find some evidence that Romans, or ancient tribes, had established forts or lookout towers or something on the site of the present Castle. I guess that must have been the romantic in me and regrettably, I was not able to find any such evidence. However, given the Castle's dominant position high above the lower reaches of the River Wharfe and the fact that Romans had a major settlement in Tadcaster, only a few miles away, plus all the information I presented in Chapter One about the Roman links to farms nearby, I would still like to believe that the Romans were at the Castle first despite a lack of evidence! Furthermore, I cannot believe that the ancients, walking up Harewood Bank from the River Wharfe along what is now the Ebor Way, would not have at least spent some time on the top of the hill, where the ruins of Harewood Castle now stand, looking down on the Wharfe valley and perhaps, who knows, looking South to Grey Stone and their eventual meeting place.

1066 to 1366

What is known about the Castle is that the ruin that we see today was, for the most part, built by Sir William Aldburgh (sometimes spelt Aldeborough and sometimes shown as de Aldeburgh) in about 1366. However, before going on to talk about this period in the history of the Castle, I will start with a brief history of the Castle from the time of William the Conqueror. The main focus of this Chapter however will be on what happened after 1366 since this is what had the biggest impact on the Castle and the clearest links to the present time.

As mentioned in Chapter Two, the manor of Harewood, held by William the Conqueror following the Norman Conquest in 1066, was granted to Robert de Romelli of Skipton Castle in about 1094. It then descended by marriage though the de Curcy (or Curci) and Fitzgerald families and after the death of Warren Fitzgerald, the manor passed through marriage to the de Redvers family and eventually to Isabel, Countess of Devon and Albemarle – the de Forz family.

By way of summary, and to attempt to make clear the 'who owned the Manor/Castle when', see the table below.

Owners of Harewood Manor/Castle from the Conquest

Dates	Owner	Number of Generations
1066 – 1094	William the Conqueror	
1094 – 1150	de Romelli (de Rumilly)	2
1150 – 1195	de Curcy (de Curci)	3
1195 – 1250	Fitzgerald	2
1250 – 1310	de Redvers	3
	de Forz (Isabel, Countess of Devon and Albemarle)	1
1310 – 1364	de Lisle	3
1364 – 1391	de Aldburgh (Aldburgh or Aldeborough)	2
1391 – 1601	Redman	6
	Ryther	9
1601 – 1641	Wentworth	2
1641 – 1656	Stafford	1
1656 – 1696	Sir John Cutler	2
1696 – 1739	John Boulter	2
1739 – present	Lascelles	9

I find it fascinating that the female descendants of de Romelli kept this name even after marriage. Robert de Romelli's daughter Cecily married William de Meschines, but Cecily and their daughters, Alice and Avicia, kept the name of de Romelli. The links between the de Romelli and de Curci families were confirmed by Kennedy[ii] who stated that,

> "the two daughters, Alice and Avicia, became joint heiresses and kept their name even after their respective marriages to Fitz Duncan ... and William de Curci ... Alice inherited the Skipton lands while Harewood went to Avicia and her husband."

In a booklet called *Harewood: A Guide*[iii], it is stated that "the Castle was built about the middle of the 12th Century by Robert de Lisle". This is a curious statement, given that whilst the original Castle was indeed built in the middle of the 12th Century, the de Lisle family did not own the Castle until the early to middle 14th Century! Robert de Lisle was allotted the manor of Harewood from his cousin Isabel, Countess of Devon and Albemarle, after protracted proceedings between various claimants, following her death in about 1310.

Robert de Lisle was summoned to parliament as Baron de Lisle of Rougemont between 1311 and 1342. According to Dennison and Richardson, who quoted from Parker (1913), "in 1337 Baron de Lisle granted the manor of Harewood to his son, also a distinguished soldier, who was created a Knight of the Garter after fighting at the battle of Crécy. Following John's death in 1355, he was succeeded by his son Robert." In terms of Rougemont Castle, "during the 13th Century the administrative centre of the manor of Harewood was at Rougemont Castle in the township of Dunkeswick, in the parish and manor of Harewood. The site of Rougemont Castle lies on the north bank of the River Wharfe, about one mile west of Harewood Bridge."[iv]

A document produced by Leeds City Council, Dept of Planning[v], in 1985, includes the following description of Rougemont Castle.

> "Rougemont Castle lies on level ground above a steep cliff on the northern bank of the River Wharfe. A large outer enclosure is surrounded by a bank and external ditch. The highest part of the enclosure, on the cliff top in the angle of the river, is enclosed by a series of wide ditches, now mostly filled in as the site lies within a dense conifer plantation. A large part of the inner enclosure has fallen into the river through erosion of the sharp river bend at this point. At least one original entrance survives in the outer enclosure, on the western side, while well-preserved ridge and furrow exists covering the eastern part. Other earthworks of uncertain form lie in the western part of the outer enclosure. The dense undergrowth makes the identification of features within both enclosures uncertain. Until Harewood Castle was built shortly after 1366, Rougemont was the administrative centre for the manor of Harewood. As no stone buildings survive on the site, it is likely that they were of timber. The plan of the earthworks and their position suggest that the mediaeval manor site may have re-used an earlier earthwork, possibly of pre-historic date."

It is worth pointing out a few linking facts between the switch from Rougemont Castle being the administrative centre to Harewood Castle.

According to Dennison and Richardson,

> "previous studies have concluded that the site on which
> Harewood Castle stands had been occupied during the 12th and
> 13th Centuries, suggesting that the existing building, which is
> generally attributed a mid to late 14th Century date, may represent
> a remodelling of an existing site. Documentary evidence indicates
> that a substantial manorial complex with stone buildings was
> located within Harewood township during the late 13th Century
> and this may have been situated on the site of the Castle. If so, it
> would appear that the administrative centre of the manor had
> moved from its earlier location at Rougemont Castle to the site of
> Harewood Castle by the late 13th Century (Moorhouse 1989, 7)."[vi]

Baron or Lord de Lisle of Rougemont's only daughter, Elizabeth, married
Sir William Aldburgh, of Aldburgh, Richmondshire.

1366 to the Present Time

Edward III granted a licence to William de Aldburgh late in 1366 to fortify (or
crenellate) his new Castle at Harewood Bank. It is nice to know that planning
permission was needed even in the 14th Century! According to Dennison and
Richardson[vii], "Sir William had held the manor of Harewood since 1364,
when Robert de Lisle paid £70 to Edward III for a licence to enfeoff[1] to de
Aldeburgh and his descendants to two parts of the manor of Harewood and
of the reversion of the third part held in dower[2] by Robert de Lisle's mother."
The Castle or fortress Sir William built was, according to Gaunt[viii] "in a form
that was rare at that period in that he avoided the old Norman conception of
a plain fortified house. Instead, he introduced many elaborations rather than
sticking to the austerity that was common in the 14th Century." Bogg[ix] stated
that "in many ways there is an Edwardian feel about it in that Aldburgh
allowed luxurious arrangements, quite different from the stern Norman
keep". He went on to say that "this change was due in some measure, to the
Magna Charta, and the great fair in the village street hard by. The inhabitants
were no longer mere serfs of the soil, but men from whom the shackles of
slavery had been loosened, and to whom, by their industry, the road to
wealth had been thrown open, so that all might freely travel upon it".[x] The
Castle is regarded as being part of the 'golden age of castle building'.

---

1. Invest with a feudal estate.
2. A widow's share for life of her husband's estate.

Mauchline[xi] made some useful links between Harewood Castle and Harewood House when she said that "in the later medieval period, although considerations of defence remained important in the north of the country, castles were increasingly residential in character, concerned with convenience, comfort and a degree of privacy. In these respects, Harewood Castle could be deemed the precursor of Lascelles's Harewood House as an assertion of personal achievement and political ambition".

Sir William Aldburgh was an officer in the court of Edward Balliol, King of Scotland if you read the work of Gaunt[xii] or a diplomat in the service of Edward Balliol, if you read the work of Mauchline[xiii] or a Messenger to the King, a civil service post of high rank and responsibility, according to Kennedy[xiv]. No matter what role Aldburgh had in the court of Balliol, one thing is certain, Edward Balliol was Edward III's puppet King of Scotland. In fact, he only managed to seize and hold the slippery throne of Scotland intermittently between 1332 and 1336 and on 20th January 1356 Balliol finally surrendered his claim to the Scottish throne to Edward III in exchange for an English pension. A website called electricscotland.com mentioned that neither historians nor the Scottish people at large, ever acknowledged Edward Balliol as one of the line of Scottish monarchs.

Above the main entrance to the Castle, and in the chapel, is the armorial crest of the founder, Sir William Aldburgh along with the badge of the deposed King of Scotland, Edward Balliol (also spelt Baliol). Illingworth[xv] stated in his writing that "Baliol died in 1363 and de Aldeborough put up his arms in the place of honour over the entrance to his new house, and again in his chapel, as a tribute to his friends memory". Dennison and Richardson[xvi], in quoting the works of Jones (1859, 136-137) and Reddyhoff (1985, 21), stated that "Balliol's coat of arms survive in several places within the castle together with those of de Aldburgh, and they also appeared on several of the items listed in the 1391 Will of Margaret de Aldburgh".

Therefore, like every other historian, it is safe to conclude that Aldburgh and Balliol were very close friends and that their armorial crests appear together in several places in the Castle. However, in relation to their friend-ship, Wade[xvii] curiously stated that "the friendship between Edward Balliol and Sir William may be reflected in the fact that the Castle was spared by the invading Scots, who, nevertheless, still sacked the Church". Kennedy[xviii] seemed to share this view stating that their friendship "may have been the factor which saved Harewood Castle from the Scottish raids which wrought great damage to other buildings in the area and elsewhere in Yorkshire, including even Harewood's Norman church". Why I find this curious is that the Scots invasion, in which the Church was badly damaged, took place in 1307, fifty seven years before Aldburgh bought the castle!

The evidence is also conclusive that Balliol died in 1363, the year before Aldburgh became owner of the Castle and two years before he was given permission to fortify it. However, where Balliol died is open to speculation. He is said by some to have died in Yorkshire (both Doncaster and Knaresborough have been mentioned) – but did he? There are also claims that he died in France, whilst others have said that he died in obscurity and that his place of death is unknown!

The family motto of the Aldburgh's, VAT SAL BE SAL, is also shown in the Castle. Bogg[xix] clearly had a sense of humour when he said that "when we read the inscription, pregnant with meaning – VAT SAL BE SAL – the literal translation of which we can interpret exactly (What Shall Be, Shall) – we are almost at a loss to know whether Aldburgh was a keen humorist or a gloomy predestinarian". The words of the chorus to the song, Que Sera, Sera, made famous by Doris Day in 1956, seem to say more of what I believe Aldburgh was trying to say than Bogg's views. The chorus is: *Que sera, sera, whatever will be, will be, the future's not ours to see, que sera, sera.*[3]

When Sir William Aldburgh died in 1388 without children, his two sisters became joint owners of the lands of Harewood. Sybil marrying Sir William Ryther, of Ryther Castle; and Elizabeth, Sir Richard Redman (sometimes spelt Redmayne) of Redman, Westmorland. The descendents of these two families inhabited the Castle jointly for nearly three centuries.

In the 16th Century, the renowned family of Gascoigne came into the possession of Harewood, from whom it passed, by the marriage of Margaret to Thomas Wentworth, grandfather of the unfortunate Earl of Strafford, who was executed on Tower Hill during the troubled time of Charles I. According to Kennedy[xx],

> "it was the Earl of Strafford's son William that inherited Harewood Castle and was forced to sell both the Castle and Gawthorp to two eminent London businessmen, Sir John

---

3. For the hardcore anoraks amongst you, the song was written by Ray Evans and Jay Livingston. The phrase came from a movie called The Barefoot Contessa in which the family motto of the Brazzi family was Che Sera, Sera. However, as more people in the United States spoke Spanish than Italian, the Che became Que when Evans and Livingston wrote their song. Finally, Doris Day first sang the song in Alfred Hitchcock's movie *The Man Who Knew Too Much.*

> Lewis and Sir John Cutler, a member of the Grocers'
> Company. Lord Strafford was so impoverished after his
> father's execution that he asked Cutler for an advance of
> £1000 on the deal in April 1658. The total price paid was
> £25,347 18s. 8d."

Whitaker (1816) as quoted by Dennison and Richardson[xxi] said that "the estate was sold to Sir John Cutler in 1656 and that the amount paid was £28,000". Although the year and the amount may be disputed, what is clear is that when the estate of Harewood was sold, the Castle was described as 'much decayed' and advertised as a "useful source of dressed stone and timber to repair the houses of the little medieval market 'town' of Harewood, with its market cross, tollbooth and butchers' shambles".[xxii]

According to Kennedy[xxiii],

> "Sir John Cutler has gone down in folklore as a miser and a hard
> landlord, satirized mercilessly by Pope[4] in *Moral Essays*[5], but the
> reputation may have been undeserved. He certainly made some
> large charitable endowments, and on a personal level was
> regarded as good coffee-house company by that most companion-
> able of men, Samuel Pepys[6], who remarked that 'his discourse was
> well worth hearing.' One thing that he was blamed for at
> Harewood was aiding the destruction of the Castle by using it as a
> source of building materials for cottages – an unfair accusation in
> view of the terms of the bill of sale."

Kennedy went on to say that "on Cutler's death the estates went to his only surviving daughter Elizabeth, Countess of Radnor, with the stipulation that if she had no children they should pass on her death to John Boulter, a Cutler kinsman. This duly happened in 1696 and Boulter appears to have redeemed Cutler's unfortunate reputation in the neighbourhood."[xxiv] In

---

4.   Alexander Pope was a famous English poet born in London on 8th June 1688.
5.   Cutler saw tenants break and houses fall; For very want, he could not build a wall. His only
     daughter in a stranger's power; For very want, he could not pay a dower.
6.   Samuel Pepys was born on 23rd February 1633 and died on 26th May 1703. As well as being
     one of the most important civil servants of his age, Pepys was a highly cultivated man, taking
     a keen interest in books, music, the theatre and science. He served on a great many committees
     and public bodies. He is most famous for the detailed private diary he kept between 1660 and
     1669, which was published after his death. The diary is one of the most important primary
     sources for the English Restoration period. It provides a fascinating combination of personal
     revelation and eyewitness accounts of great events, such as the Great Plague of London (1665)
     and the Great Fire of London (1666).

other words, he was seen to be very generous.

It was Boulter's son Edmund who was forced by debt to sell the manor in 1739 to Henry Lascelles. Upon the death of Henry Lascelles in 1753 the estate passed to his son Edwin (1712-1795). As we will see in the next Chapter, Edwin, who was created Baron or Lord Harewood in 1790, was responsible for building the present Harewood House and was also responsible for transforming the landscape of the new house with the help of the famous Capability Brown.

The Castle remained isolated until being taken into the Pleasure Grounds in around 1813. During alterations at that time, "indications of previous gardens were uncovered, showing that the Castle area was from the beginning a planned layout. Gardens on the east and west sides of the walls descended in terraces down the steep slope to the River Wharfe and, on the level ground below, a large fish pond was located." [xxv]

There is no doubt that road construction (the new road in 1799 climbed Harewood Bank and its successor the A61), would have had a damaging impact on the Castle and its grounds.

The Interior

In its heyday, the interior of the Castle must have been very grand.

The Will of Margaret de Aldburgh in 1391 (referred to earlier) is said to have listed at least seven beds with elaborate bedclothes, together with tapestries and cushions (with the arms of both Aldburgh and Balliol), plus plates, armour and clothing.

Bogg[xxvi] also gave the following description:

> "The grand entrance portal on the east is high enough for a man to enter on horseback. This entrance was defended by a portcullis, above which was a chapel. The internal passages in the walls are admirably arranged and run through the whole building, forming a safe means of escape from any portions of the building. On the west side of the Great Hall is a canopied recess, not unlike a tomb; it is a beautiful late Edwardian recessed sideboard."

Let us now turn to the Castle today.

Conservation of the Castle

In its document detailing the *Ancient Monuments in Leeds*, referred to earlier, Leeds City Council included the following description of the Castle in 1985[xxvii].

> "The main part of the structure survives to eaves level essentially as built in the mid-14th Century, but is lacking floors and roof. Rectangular in plan, the building has three levels and a basement with a principal access at ground floor level on the east and a secondary entrance on the west. An ornately decorated wall cupboard, or aumbrey, survives in the northern wall".

As one would expect, after centuries of neglect and weathering taking its toll, the Castle was in great danger of becoming totally unstable and perhaps even collapsing. As a result it became a Grade I listed Castle and was placed on the register of Buildings at Risk by English Heritage. It is unlikely that much within the Castle ruins would have changed from the 1985 description above at the point when it was saved from further damage and decay in 2000 by a £1m rescue plan funded partly by English Heritage and partly by the Harewood Estate, with money that Yorkshire TV paid for the building of the Emmerdale Village. In 2004 the scaffolding went up and the main contractors, Historic Property Restoration of Newcastle, went in to stabilise the Castle and perhaps prepare it for life as a visitor attraction once again. It was never planned that the Castle would be restored, only preserved. In other words, to stabilise the building to make it safe, and to try to keep at bay things like ivy that would cause further destruction to the stone work and so on.

This, of course, was not anywhere near as straight-forward as it sounds. Restoration of the Castle required careful and coordinated efforts from builders, architects, archaeologists, historians, botanists, zoologists, geologists, structural engineers, ecologists, staff of the Harewood Estate, Historic Property Restoration and English Heritage. At times, the demands between this group of professionals were in conflict. For example, it might be agreed that a particular wall might need to be repaired but what, exactly, was nesting within the walls that could be killed in the making-good process and would have to be rescued first? Or, yes, scaffolding needs to be placed on the pile of rubble at the bottom of a wall but what, say the historians or archaeologists is hidden beneath the pile of rubble?

In July 2005 Harewood Castle was taken off the Buildings at Risk register.

According to a *Yorkshire Post* article[xxviii], during the restoration process the Castle had been "photogrammatically recorded, two photographs taken at the same time using a specialised camera and merged to create a stone-by-stone drawing of the structure. The less accessible areas were drawn by hand". The next stage is for the Harewood Estate to decide how the public might be able to visit the Castle, since the funding included conditions such as allowing controlled public access. Christopher Ussher, Resident Agent of Harewood Estate, was quoted in the *Yorkshire Post* article as saying "we hope that we will not only be able to take people to the Castle, but offer 'off site' access and interpretation through the use of computer technology as well."

In speaking to Christopher Ussher and Lord Lascelles in the Autumn of 2006, they both acknowledged that they would like to be able to offer patrons of Harewood House some type of very limited access to Harewood Castle but equally they acknowledged just how very difficult it would be to do so. As Lord Harewood pointed out in a later interview, "no one goes by the Castle, you have to go to it and doing so is extremely difficult".

End Notes

i   Edmund Bogg, *Lower Wharfeland* (1904), p 375.
ii   Carol Kennedy, *Harewood: The Life and Times of an English Country House* (1982), p22.
iii   Harewood House Trust, *Harewood: A Guide*, p 10.
iv   Ed Dennison and S Richardson, *Harewood Castle, Harewood, West Yorkshire: An Archaeological and Architectural Condition Survey* (unpublished EDAS report for Harewood Estate) (forthcoming), p 2.
v   Leeds City Council, Dept of Planning, *Ancient Monuments in Leeds* (1985), p 10.
vi   Dennison and Richardson, op cit, p 2.
vii   Ibid, p 2.
viii   Arthur Gaunt, *History, People and Places in Yorkshire* (1975), p 84.
ix   Bogg, op cit, p 374.
x   Ibid, p 374.
xi   Mary Mauchline, *Harewood House* (1992), p 14.
xii   Gaunt, op cit, p 85.
xiii   Mauchline, op cit, p 14.
xiv   Kennedy, op cit, p 23.
xv   John Illingworth, *Yorkshire's Ruined Castle* (1970), p 139.
xvi   Denison and Richardson, op cit, p 3.
xvii   Ron Wade, *Vat Sal Be Sal* (1982), p 10.
xviii   Kennedy, op cit, p 23.
xix   Bogg, op cit, p 375.
xx   Kennedy, op cit, p 26.
xxi   Dennison and Richardson, op cit, p 3.
xxii   Mauchline, op cit, p 14.
xxiii   Kennedy, op cit, p 26.
xxiv   Ibid, p 26.
xxv   Mauchline, op cit, pp 14 and 15.

xxvi   Bogg, op cit, p 375.
xxvii   Leeds City Council, op cit, pp 9 and 10.
xxviii Yorkshire Post article dated 30th July 2005.

CHAPTER FIVE
Harewood House and the Lascelles

Harewood House

Introduction

In many respects this Chapter was the most difficult to write. Firstly, from a researcher's or historian's point of view it was not the shortage of information that was the problem, it was having too much! There is almost a limitless amount written in one form or another, including various websites, about Harewood House. Secondly, as this is a book about Harewood in general and not exclusively about Harewood House, it was difficult to decide what should be included by way of an overview of the House to give you a feel for it, without going into too much detail. Also, no history of the House would be complete without including information about the fascinating family who built it, the Lascelles. Therefore, I have included what I regard as essential information in order to give you some insights into this remarkable family. Anyway, I hope that I have been able to offer someone new to the House and the Lascelles family, sufficient information that whets their appetite to visit Harewood House and/or to read one of the excellent guides or books written about the House and its illustrious owners.

Without doubt, Harewood House puts Harewood on the map. It offers many attractions and events that draw visitors from all over the world during the very busy season, currently from March to the end of November. Even outside the normal 'tourist' season, there are concerts and other events that keep Harewood House in the minds of people. The House and the vast Estate offer employment to a considerable number of people, including locals, and provides housing for both current and former employees. However, there is inevitably a downside to living on the doorstep of a major tourist attraction – tourists! Not that there is anything wrong with tourists, but the sheer numbers attending some of the more popular events causes major traffic problems on the already busy A61 and the A659. Also, roads such as Church Lane, the main exit route for traffic to Harrogate, become completely gridlocked during certain events. However, some locals try to overcome these problems by not leaving their houses, at least by car, during those busy times. In general, I suspect that most locals will feel, as I do, that where we live, including the fantastic countryside that surrounds the village, is so special that the inconveniences caused at times by Harewood House are insignificant by comparison to the benefits of living in such a beautiful place.

Although I have already said that Harewood House puts Harewood on the map, and clearly has a significant impact on the village itself, that, of course, has not always been the case. From an historic point of view, Harewood House is relatively new! After all, the recorded history of the village goes back to the Norman Conquest, and before, but Harewood House has only been in existence since the 18th Century! In fact, the House was only completed in 1771.

The main focus of this Chapter is obviously Harewood House. However, the Harewood 'experience' is far more than simply the House itself, it also includes the natural beauty of the Yorkshire countryside, enhanced by Capability Brown[1] and later by Humphrey Repton[2].

---

1.   Lancelot became known as 'Capability' because of his habit of saying: 'I see great capability of improvement here.' According to Jones (1859, p 187), he was born in Northumberland in 1715 and from his beginnings as a kitchen gardener, he raised himself to the highest pinnacle of fame as a landscape gardener and improver of grounds and was regarded as 'the oracle of taste'. He also acquired a reputation as an architect and erected several mansions for the

Quite frankly, I could not find better description of the grounds of the Harewood Estate (the park) than those of Bogg[i] written in 1892. Whilst Bogg's 1904 version is wonderfully written as well, his 1892 version is by far the most picturesque.

> "Although the park is famed for its beauty, yet we shall never forget the glorious scene of nature's loveliness viewed from its outskirts. The vale is sweetly undulating and covered with rich pasture, the circling dome of the opposite hills forming a splendid background, tracing their bold outlines on the sky, and, as the sun sweeps down the western hills, diffusing rays of golden light and tips village church and spire with her magic wand, the silvery meanderings of the old Wharfe flash and sparkle like a dream of beauty; the scene at such a time presents a combination of nature's loveliness scarcely equalled and never excelled. Entering the road we drop down to the bridge, a massive structure of four arches, built at different periods. A stone in the wall bears the following inscription: *this bridge was built by the county, 1729.*"

What a gifted, descriptive and romantic writer Bogg was.

Now, let us go back in history to discover the roots of Harewood House, including its owners with their Royal connections.

The Lascelles

In this Chapter I will go back hundreds of years to tell the story of both the Lascelles and Harewood House itself. However, I will begin this section about the Lascelles by quoting from a relatively contemporary author who wrote her book only 25 years ago! Carol Kennedy, in the first paragraph of

---

nobility. His arrangement of plantations, pleasure gardens and so on at Harewood is generally considered one of his best undertakings, and is regarded as a model in several works on landscape gardening.

2.   Humphrey Repton was born in Bury St Edmonds in 1752 and died in 1818. He was determined to be the successor to Capability Brown and at Harewood he most certainly was. At Harewood Repton went beyond the scope of Brown to include a vision of the House itself and its place in the landscape that surrounded it. Indeed, Repton is credited with coining the term 'landscape garden' to describe the natural style of gardening which he felt required 'the united powers of the landscape painter and the practical gardener'. At Harewood Repton added vitality and softened the outlines of the vista to the south without destroying the original concept of the Harewood landscape as created by Brown and Edwin Lascelles.

her excellent book about Harewood (*Harewood: The Life and Times of an English Country House*), states that when the present Earl, George Lascelles,

> "wakes in his lofty, north-facing bedroom high up under the parapet of Harewood House, he can look out over a sweep of parkland and rolling West Yorkshire dale country outwardly little changed from the view that six generations of his forebears enjoyed."

These words were written less than 30 years ago, and there has still been little change to the views. However, in other ways the speed of change for the Earl, his family and Harewood House has been astronomical. Now, let us go back in history to find out more about the fascinating story of the Lascelles.

Let us begin by establishing where the name 'Lascelles' came from. According to Bogg[ii] "in the province of Touraine, in France, is a village named Lassele, from which it is supposed this family received their name. Amongst the retainers or knights composing the train of Alan, Earl of Richmond, who commanded the rear-guard of the army at the battle of Hastings, was one Picot de Lascells. For his share in the Conquest, he later received the Manor of Scruton, North Yorkshire."[3]

Kennedy[iii] made the point that the first of the Harewood line turns up in the records of 1315. This information was confirmed by a reference on the Genuki website in which it was stated that the family of the Lascelles is very ancient, and appears from a pedigree in Loidis et Elmet[4], to have descended from John de Lascelles, of Hinderskelfe who had held lands in 1315. Hinderskelfe or 'Hundred Hill' was built by the Baron of Greystock[5] and when it was burnt down, Castle Howard was erected on its site. In

---

3. Genuki. In the Domesday Book, Scruton, near Northallerton, was called Scurveton and Scaruton. At the time of the Conquest Cnut and Torfin held two manors here, but when the Survey was made their lands had been transferred to Picot, one of Earl Alan's men, whose name was written in later times as Pygot and Pigot. The manor subsequently passed, probably by marriage, to the Lascelles, and was in the possession of that family when Kirby's Inquest was taken in 1277.
4. The term Loidis is the ancient name for Leeds. Elmete refers to the ancient Celtic-British Kingdom of Elmete. More information appears in Chapter One of this book: Harewood before 1066. 'Loidis et Elmet' refers to information that was documented within the region of Leeds in the Kingdom of Elmet.
5. Wikipedia. The title Baron Greystock (or Greystoke) has been created twice in the Peerage of England. It was first created when John de Greystock was summoned to parliament in 1295 and it became extinct on his death. It was next created by Sir Ralph de Greystock in 1321, and went into abeyance in 1569, after passing into the Dacre family.

Harewood: A Guide[iv], the family moved from Hinderskelfe to Northallerton and Francis Lascelles (1612-1667) was Colonel in the Parliamentary Army and later MP (1653) for the North Riding of Yorkshire, a tradition carried on by many of his descendants for over 200 years. The move to Northallerton seems to have come from the marriage to a girl from that area. Francis Lascelles was the grandfather of Henry Lascelles (1690-1753).

Henry made his fortune in Barbados, handling government contracts and from his own dealings with sugar planters, mainly lending them money. Whilst this statement is true, it hardly does justice to the fascinating story behind the Lascelles family and its links to the Caribbean that lasted for no fewer than 327[6] years! For this reason I decided to devote the next section of this Chapter to this extraordinary story. For now, however, I will return to the overview of the Lascelles and its links to Harewood.

In 1739 both the Estates of Gawthorpe and Harewood came up for sale and Henry Lascelles bought them. The two Estates were sold by the Boulters family to clear their debts.

> "The two estates with their townships and tenants and the manor house itself, Old Gawthorpe Hall, were valued for sale at £63,827. The estate was ideally situated; within easy reach of Northallerton and the North Riding, where the Lascelles had long-established roots, and only eight miles from the burgeoning new industrial centre of Leeds. It was also within twenty miles of York with all its fashionable diversions of shops, assembly room and the new racecourse."[v]

Henry's son, Edwin Lascelles (1712-1795), was born in Barbados, along with his cousin, Edward Lascelles (1740-1820) – it was Edward who eventually inherited the Estates from Edwin and who was made the first Earl of Harewood in 1812, "establishing the dynasty that continues to flourish seven generations on."[vi]

If we bring things forward through many generations of the Lascelles 'dynasty', the current Earl, the 7th, is George Lascelles who was born in 1923. His father Henry Lascelles (1882-1947) married HRH Princess Mary (who would later become The Princess Royal), daughter of King George V in 1922.

---

6. According to *Harewood: A Guide*, the Lascelles only relinquished their final links with Barbados in the 1970s.

It is more than slightly confusing to try to keep straight in one's head exactly which Henry Lascelles we might be talking about given that there have been no fewer than five Earls of Harewood with the same name, not forgetting, of course, Henry Lascelles (1690-1753) who bought the Estate in the first place in 1739, but who was not one of the Earls! For the record:

- 1st Earl (1740-1820) Edward
- 2nd Earl (1767-1841) Henry (1)
- 3rd Earl (1797-1857) Henry (2)
- 4th Earl (1824-1892) Henry (3)
- 5th Earl (1846-1929) Henry (4)
- 6th Earl (1882-1947) Henry (5)
- 7th Earl (1923 -) George.

As I started this section with information about the 7th Earl it seems appropriate to end with a quote from one of the Earl's son's, David Lascelles (the eldest son of the Earl and, as such, has the title of Viscount), written in *Harewood: A Guide.*[vii]

> "We often use the word 'continuum' when talking about what we're trying to achieve here. By this we mean that, although we are keenly aware of Harewood's history, we do not see our role as being simply to preserve that history in aspic, but to deal with the present and look to the future with the same spirit of enterprise and sense of excellence that was in action when Harewood was first built. So Harewood must continue to re-invent itself. The House is now run as a charitable Trust, able to attract public funds from English Heritage and the European Community, one of the first privately-run stately homes in Britain to achieve museum status. These are just the means, however. The end is something more ambitious: not simply to look after a beautiful and tranquil piece of England but to make sure it continues to be somewhere truly alive and exciting and modern, looking forward with eagerness as well as looking back with respect."

For this book, I interviewed David Lascelles in November 2006. During our discussion he made many of the points raised above, which indicates to me that he not only has a long-term vision for Harewood, which has not changed very much over the past twenty five years, but he is actively working towards his vision. In fact, the vision seems to have come more clearly into focus and some of it has already been realised, given the various changes that have occurred over the past two decades plus.

The Lascelles and their Links to the British Atlantic

Given that 2007 marks the 200th anniversary of the passing of the Act of Emancipation which ultimately led to the abolishment of slavery, and for which William Wilberforce will always be remembered, devoting a few pages to this important chapter in the life of the Lascelles and British history in general seems both timely and significant.

The information within this section is taken from the excellent book written by Dr Simon Smith of the University of York in 2006 entitled *Slavery, Family and Gentry Capitalism in the British Atlantic: The World of the Lascelles, 1648-1834*[7]. It also contains information from an article downloaded from the BBC website entitled *Slavery and Harewood House*, also written by Simon Smith.

The Harewood Trust and the University of York
The link between the Lascelles, the Harewood Trust and the University of York began in 1998 and is a fascinating story in itself. When Harewood House Trust was established in 1986 it began the process of taking an inventory of what has been described by many authors as a 'treasure house'. The Trust came upon a black metal box containing West Indian papers, including details of several plantations. Furthermore, during the recataloguing of Harewood artefacts, more manuscripts were discovered in a locked bureau. As the Trust was keen to establish the family's past connections with slavery, and to put the finds into context, it sought guidance from historians working at the University of York. At about the same time, Harewood Trust received designated museum status which stimulated research into Harewood House and its collections. One of the projects sponsored by the Trust was a study of the involvement of the Lascelles in Caribbean trade and slavery. Smith[viii] pointed out that "consciously or subconsciously, social and political events in Britain and the wider world influenced the Trust's decision to adopt a policy of openness about Harewood's past links with slavery". This marked the launch of the research which ultimately ended with the publication of the Smith book.

Vast fortunes were gained and lost during the 18th Century in trade in the West Indies and during this time millions of Africans were transported

---

7. The term 'gentry capitalism' is used to describe the institutional structures of trade and finance underpinning the growth of Atlantic trade during the 18th Century. Further, it refers to families who were already landed and respectable yet which attempted to increase their wealth and influence through colonial trade. (Smith, 2006, p 9)

across the Atlantic to be sold as slaves. In the Smith book, he used the Lascelles family as a focus during his investigations as Henry Lascelles (1690-1753) in particular emerged as one of the most successful businessmen of this period in history.

Yorkshire was only the Starting Point for the Lascelles
Smith pointed out that the Lascelles' business empire extended throughout large parts of Britain. In addition, although the Lascelles' most significant commercial connection was with Barbados, they also had links with other islands in the West Indies (including Antigua, Jamaica and Tobago) together with business interests in North America and South East Asia. During much of the time that the Lascelles were involved in the West Indies, their ships plied back and forth across the Atlantic with their cargoes of slaves, dry goods, sugar, rum and other provisions.

The Journey to Land Ownership
Despite their involvement in Atlantic trade, the Lascelles owned very little property in the West Indies until after the American Revolution (1775-1783). Apart from the shipping business, the Lascelles had also made a great deal of money making loans to plantation owners in the West Indies. The financial problems which followed the Revolution led to many owners defaulting on their loans and surrendering their property to creditors. As a result, the Lascelles family acquired a huge property portfolio. In the BBC website article[ix] Smith states that, "between 1773 and 1787, more than 27,000 acres and 2,947 slaves were acquired, worth £293,000 (about £28.3 million today)". Given that the American Revolution did not begin until 1775, it would appear, given the information contained in the Smith article, that the build-up to the war also caused hardship to the plantation owners and thus forced some of them to default on their loans.

327 Years Associated with the Caribbean
As mentioned earlier, the Lascelles' links to the Caribbean lasted for over 300 years, beginning in 1648 and ending when the last plantation was sold in 1975. Their involvement in the sugar trade is said to have begun around 1680, they owned plantations continually for over 200 years and they were tied to the same London commission house of Lascelles and Maxwell, Mark Lane, City of London, until 1954. This continuity allowed Smith an invaluable opportunity to investigate the development of the British Atlantic economy from a political, social and economic perspective.

Henry the Barbados Merchant
Henry returned to London following the death of his older brother George

in 1729 and left his half-brother Edward to run the Barbadian side of the family business. Henry returned briefly to Barbados and married his second wife there in 1731, but returned permanently to London by March 1732. As an MP, he argued in favour of a significant piece of legislation: An Act for the more easy recovery of Debts in His Majesty's Plantations and Colonies in America.

According to Smith[x], "by the early 1730s, Henry Lascelles was established as a leading West Indian trader and the head of an ascendant gentry family. The ambitious commercial projects he now launched upon elevated himself into a super-merchant and set the Lascelles on the path to Aristocratic eminence".

The Five Sources of Henry's Immense Wealth

The first of Henry's projects was taking over the commission house business following the death of his brother George. The main business of the commission house was to receive and then sell on the cargoes sent by planters to London, including sugar and rum, and in addition organising shipments of goods being sent back to the plantations. Henry formed a partnership with George Maxwell (of Edinburgh and Barbados) creating the 'Lascelles and Maxwell' commission house in London in 1743.

The second source of wealth came from government contracts for the supply of provisions and stores to the armed forces.

The third important project was involvement in the slave trade. Henry and his brother Edward had invested in this area whilst on Barbados. Following his return to London, Henry looked to transfer the skills acquired as a shipper and trader in goods, to the shipment of slaves. The consortium he formed with other traders invested in ships which delivered supplies and collected slaves off the coast of Guinea. The consortium worked with the agreement of the local rulers. In addition to transporting slaves, other cargo included elephants' teeth, gold and gold dust, guinea corn, gum and malaguetta[8]. According to the BBC article[xi], between 1736 and 1744, a total of about £41,200 (approximately £4.5 million today) was invested and upwards of twelve ships are known to have engaged in this trade.

Henry's fourth source of income came from part-ownership of ships, which

---

8.   A type of pepper (Amomum melegueta), also called 'grains of paradise', 'Guinea grains' or 'alligator pepper'. In the 18th Century, the part of West Africa where Malaguetta pepper was grown was commonly known as the Pepper Coast or Malaguetta Coast.

was a common practice amongst merchants at the time in order to spread their risks. In addition to the ships previously mentioned, by his death in 1753, Henry was a part owner of no fewer than twenty one ships.

Henry's fifth business interest was in money lending, to Barbados planters in the main. As mentioned earlier, whilst this business was started by Henry, it continued long after his death and was a key factor in the growth of the Lascelles' property portfolio.

There is no doubt that Henry was a successful and respected businessman, but he also had enemies and there were accusations of corruption, as we will see later in this section. It is also worth mentioning that by the time of Henry's death in 1753, he ceased to hold contracts for the provision of supplies and had scaled back his involvement in the slave trade.

The Death of Henry Lascelles
'Deaths: Henry Lascelles, Esq; a very great Barbados merchant, and sometime member of parliament for Northallerton.'

According to Smith[xii], "Henry's obituary in the *London Magazine* emphasises the key achievements in the eyes of his peers: the extent of his business interests as a merchant, his immense wealth, his political standing as an MP, and his claim to gentility but lack of titled status." Smith went on to say that whilst the obituary had not included any details about how Henry died, shortly afterwards a Yorkshire diarist, Thomas Gyll, is said to have reported that 'an account came from London of the death of old Mr Lascelles, who was reported to have cut his throat and arms and across his belly'.

Why Henry Lascelles should commit suicide is a complete mystery. From a financial point of view, at the time of his death he was one of the richest men in Britain; with net assets totalling in the region of £408,000, which would be approximately £52 million today[xiii]. Politically he was well respected and successful. As Smith[xiv] pointed out, "of Henry Lascelles' physical and mental state, little can be said with certainty" and "his complex business affairs must have exerted an immense strain on his mind and body over many years. In the end, perhaps Lascelles paid the ultimate price for the great fortune he raised through his unrelenting drive and ambition".

Despite the fact that Henry was believed to have committed suicide, he still had a Christian burial at All Saints in Northallerton. It is interesting to note, however, that there is no gravestone recognition of this although the names of his father, twin sister and first wife are all set in the floor in the nave of the Church. There is also nothing on show at Harewood House which commemorates the creator of the family's wealth.

Henry Lascelles' notorious career, and the mysterious way in which he died, were not quickly forgotten. For as Smith[xv] pointed out,

> "More than forty years after his death, the diarist Joseph Farington recalled how 'Mr Lascelles, the Father of the late Lord Harewood, of Daniel Lascelles, and of General Lascelles killed himself by opening the veins in his wrists', and how the same Henry Lascelles had been accused of extortion and corruption, primarily in relation to the role of Customs Collector. Two decades later, in 1814, Henry's notoriety was similarly recalled when a small vault in the south transept of Northallerton church was opened, exposing his lead-lined coffin. On this occasion, Lascelles was remembered as 'one of those unprincipled men who were concerned in the shameful South Sea business, whereby he amassed great wealth to the ruin of many'. A corpse cannot defend itself and no evidence has been found to substantiate a charge that the deceased never had to face in his lifetime. Nevertheless, the readiness of the annalist to speak ill of such a long-dead Northallerton MP provides further indication of Henry's grim posthumous reputation."

Was Henry's Death Really Suicide?
I know that far too many people today seem to jump on the 'conspiracy theory' bandwagon every time there is a death that cannot be explained but, in the case of Henry Lascelles, perhaps we need to think again. In the cold light of day, and 254 years after the event, perhaps it is time to take another look at the facts or information that is known to us and to decide for ourselves whether or not his death was, in fact, suicide or murder. Let us now examine what is known from both perspectives and try to establish what the motives might have been.

From the research of Simon Smith and his colleagues from the University of York, Henry Lascelles seemed to have everything to live for. He was obviously enormously wealthy and was an extremely successful, innovative businessman. He was well connected in extremely high places in many countries, but especially in the United Kingdom and Barbados. He was a well respected, albeit at times extremely controversial, politician. He seemed to be extremely confident and self-satisfied. He had split his empire into two and given the 'trade' part to his son Daniel Lascelles (1714-1784), based in Barbados and London, and the 'landed gentry' part to his son Edwin Lascelles (1712-1795), based at Harewood. There was nothing mentioned by Smith about Henry suffering from ill health, including depression, and no reference to a suicide note being left by Henry.

Given this 'evidence' what on earth could the motive have been for Henry to have taken his own life? Perhaps he was very ill, but kept the fact from his family, or he was feeling guilty about the manner in which he made some of his money. Quite frankly, the latter potential motive does not really seem to stack up, given Henry's drive and extreme confidence in himself, and his own personal business ethics. Perhaps he did have a life threatening illness, but did people have such forewarning 254 years ago? On balance, the motives for dying by his own hand seem quite thin unless, of course, there is some evidence somewhere yet to be discovered. However, given the passage of time, and the fact that the Harewood Estate gave Simon Smith and his team carte blanche to search wherever they wished, including complete access to any papers the Estate had, I suspect that no further evidence will ever be unearthed except, perhaps, from family papers that will always remain secret, or information passed to family members that has never been recorded. I added this last bit of speculation because Henry's family certainly gave the impression, via Smith's writing, that they accepted the fact that Henry had taken his own life. Further, at the time perhaps they felt guilty or ashamed to admit it as they seemed to go out of their way to distance themselves from him. As a result, there was no mention of him at the family burial place at All Saints Church, Northallerton, nor at Harewood House. Have the family simply been far too hard and unforgiving of Henry for all these years or is there further evidence that we simply will never know?

Now, what about the case for murder? Henry Lascelles was the Richard Branson or Rupert Murdoch or Bill Gates of his time, perhaps even more so. Successful people very often make enemies. From all accounts, Henry Lascelles had a tremendous number of enemies. Some fellow businessmen were simply jealous of just how successful and entrepreneurial Henry was. If there was a business opportunity, it seems that Henry was one of the first to spot it and to take full advantage of it. I suspect that Henry would have driven certain people out of business, and this makes enemies. There had been accusations of corruption against Henry and his brother, especially with regard to the Customs job in Barbados. However, whilst there was apparently some evidence to substantiate this charge, Smith seemed to conclude that the business ethics of the time were not what they are today and there were far fewer governmental controls then. Therefore, it seems that neither Henry nor his brother Edward were doing anything different from other businessmen at the time. Our concept of 'you cannot prove your innocence through pointing out other people's guilt', did not seem to apply in the middle of the 18th Century.

Henry was very astute when it came to understanding who to support, and when, with regard to both politicians and those associated with the monarchy. He expected to be recognised, and rewarded, by those he supported, both financially and psychologically, and he was, handsomely. Some people would see this as being corrupt, especially those who backed the wrong side, or did so at the wrong time. From what Smith was able to unearth, some of Henry's enemies were extremely outspoken and some even seemed to have a vendetta against him. Would an individual, or group of individuals, hate Henry to such an extent that they would murder him? This is unlikely to be the case today, given that the most outspoken would be the first to be accused if anything happened to their sworn enemy. However, perhaps that was not the case 254 years ago. I might be wrong, but I suspect, that crime detection basically did not exist back then. So, perhaps one of his enemies did, in fact, either commit murder or got someone else to murder him.

From all that I have just mentioned, could one conclude that Henry did, in fact, take his own life or was murdered? Of course not. If I was a presiding judge trying to establish both motive and likely cause, I would have to give an 'open verdict'. If my 'judgement' is the correct one, then I personally think that it would be appropriate for Henry to be recognised in some way at Harewood House for being the father of the Lascelles/Harewood 'dynasty'. After all, if it had not been for Henry, Harewood House would not exist.

The Lascelles after the Death of Henry in 1753
Henry had divided his fortune to deliberately separate the English and West Indian sections, leaving his son Daniel Lascelles (1714-1784) as head of the business interests, with Edwin Lascelles (1712-1795) being able to assume the role of aspiring aristocrat. The BBC website pointed out that "a Cambridge University education was followed by a Grand Tour of Europe. After earning an honourable discharge for his role in the defeat of the Jacobites (1745), Edwin entered parliament as MP for Scarborough and by 1748 was installed as Lord of the Manor of Harewood."[xvi] The death of Daniel in 1784 and his younger brother Henry in 1786, both without heirs, reunited the family fortune. Smith speculated that if Edwin had not inherited from his brothers, the future Earls of Harewood would most likely have severed their connections with slavery completely and it is true to say that at the time of the construction of Harewood House (1759-1771), Edwin owned neither slaves nor plantations.

Upon Edwin's own death in 1795, the Harewood Estate passed to his cousin, Edward Lascelles (1740-1820), who would later become the 1st Earl of Harewood.

Post-Slavery

Following the debates which finally led to emancipation, the British Government agreed to pay compensation to former owners. In 1836, Henry Lascelles (1767-1841), the 2nd Earl of Harewood still had six properties in Barbados and Jamaica with 1,277 slaves and approximately 3,250 acres of land. He was awarded a total compensation of £23,309 (which would be approximately £2 million today), for freeing his former slaves. Whilst, this money helped in the rationalisation of the Lascelles' West Indian interests, it did not mark the end of their involvement as absentee plantation owners.

The Earls of Harewood were quick to embrace new approaches to estate management and plantation agriculture in the West Indies. The same could be said about how the Harewood Estate in Yorkshire has been run over the centuries. They continually sought to find new ways to grow sugar cane, they attempted crop diversification, sold their least productive plantations, merged estates and combined workforces in order to try to ensure maximum productivity. A key to their success as absentee landlords was the establishment of an accountancy system which reduced fraud and helped to detect poor performance on the part of both attorneys and estate managers.

As mentioned earlier, the Lascelles' links to the Caribbean finally ended when the last plantation was sold in 1975. However, the history of the family's connection with the West Indies is still developing – for example, with its own recognition of the abolition of slavery through hosting the Carnival Messiah in September 2007.

I will now return to the Yorkshire history of the Lascelles.

Gawthorpe Hall

I thought it would be interesting to offer the words that appeared in an advertisement for Gawthorp(e) Hall in 1656, more than 80 years prior to Henry Lascelles buying the Hall, along with the Harewood Estate. The information came from Bogg's 1892 book[xvii] and the spelling is as it is said to have appeared in the advertisement!

"Gawthorp Hall, most part of the walles built with good stone and all the honses covered with slate, and a great part of that new building, four rooms in the onld building, all waynscotted[9], fyve large roomes in the new building all waynscotted, likewise and colored like wallnut tree, tile matereals of which house, if sould, would raise 500l at least. To this belongeth a park, in former tymes stored with deere a park-like place it is, and a brook running through the middle of it, which turnes 4 payer of millstones att 2 milles. The stank, or pond, at Gawthorp, is well stored with trout, roch, gudgeon and eyles."

As one might guess, the history of Gawthorpe Hall, and its illustrious owners, goes back many, many centuries. In linking Gawthorpe Hall and Harewood, several family names will be included that have already appeared. Kennedy[xviii] mentioned that

"descendants of the Redmans held Harewood for seven genera-tions, those of the Rythers for nine. The Redmans, meanwhile, married several times into the Gascoigne family, whose estate bordered Harewood and whose home was a medieval manor house called Gawthorpe Hall. Its situation was about 350 yards south of where Harewood House now stands, and its founda-tions, for it were pulled down by Edwin Lascelles in 1759 to build his fine new mansion, lie under Capability Brown's lake in the park".[10]

In the time of Queen Elizabeth I, the Estates of Harewood and Gawthorpe came together when Margaret Gascoigne married Thomas Wentworth. As we saw in the last Chapter, their ill-fated grandson became the Earl of Strafford, impeached and beheaded for treason during the Long Parliament of Charles I. Strafford's son William inherited Gawthorpe, Harewood Castle

---

9.   Free Online Dictionary. The word appears to be wainscot which means the panel forming the lower part of an interior wall when it is finished differently from the rest or wooden panelling used to line the walls of a room.

10.   Whilst it is true that the remains of Gawthorpe Hall lie under the lake and that its location is, by all accounts correct, Kennedy's information gives the impression that the Old Hall was pulled down in 1759. However, further research shows that during the time that Harewood House (called New Gawthorpe Hall during its construction) was being built, between 1759 and 1771, the Lascelles remained in Gawthorpe Hall. Also, although several authors have stated that Old Gawthorpe Hall was pulled down in 1771, Mary Mauchline stated that the old house was not pulled down until 1776. In fact, the house steward at the time, Samuel Popplewell, is reputed to have said that he was delighted when the old house was finally pulled down in 1776 because he was getting tired of looking at the ruins!

and the rest of the Estates but in 1656 was forced to sell them, for financial reasons, to two London businessmen, Sir John Lewis and Sir John Cutler. Presumably, the advertisement mentioned at the beginning of this section is what enticed Lewis and Cutler to buy the Estate. The Estate eventually passed from Cutler to his kinsman, John Boulter. (Although the Cutler Estate passed directly to his daughter Elizabeth, it was stipulated that if she should die childless, the Estate was to be passed on to Boulter.) Closing the circle, as mentioned earlier in this Chapter, it was the Boulter family who sold the Estate to Henry Lascelles in 1739.

Although Edwin Lascelles, who inherited the Estates of Gawthorpe and Harewood in 1753, made improvements to Gawthorpe Hall by adding a portico and remodelling and redecorating, he had already "resolved to rebuild on a spot rather elevated above that of old Gawthorp . . . which commanded a rich home view over fields and woods".[xix]

Harewood House

The building of Edwin Lascelles's new house called for the services of the leading architects, decorators and cabinetmakers of their time, including: John Carr,[11] Robert Adam,[12] Thomas Chippendale (more about him later), Joseph Ross (some authors refer to Joseph Rose II or Joseph Rose Jr), Angelica Kauffmann (a Swiss-born decorator who is said to have taken London by storm) and Antonio Zucchi (who became Kauffmann's second husband in 1781). John Carr had an extremely able 'partner' in the building of Harewood House, John Muschamp and his son of Harewood. The foundation stone was laid on 23rd March 1759 by Edwin Lascelles himself.

In terms of further information about John Carr, Linstrum[xx] mentioned that he was introduced to Edwin Lascelles by Stephen Thompson of Kirby Hall[13] as early as 1748, as a builder who could make plans, and the new stables at Old Gawthorp (later Harewood) were designed by John Carr and

---

11.　According to Jones (1859, p 185), John Carr was born at Horbury, near Wakefield in 1721. He was twice Lord Mayor of York and rose to the highest eminence as an architect. He erected many stately mansions, and other public buildings in Yorkshire and adjoining counties. Harewood House is one of his best works. He died at his residence, Askham Hall, Yorkshire on 22 February 1807.

12.　Robert Adam, a celebrated Scottish architect was born at Kirkcaldy in Fifeshire in 1728. He speedily rose to great eminence in his profession. In November 1761, under the reign of George III, Adam was appointed, jointly with William Chambers, as Architect of the King's Works. He was returned MP for the county of Kinross in 1768 and died in 1792. He is interred in Westminster Abbey.

built by him and his father, Robert. You may find it interesting to note that the stables built by John and Robert Carr have been used for many years as a restaurant, shop and access to the bird gardens in the grounds of Harewood House. Unfortunately, they had been deteriorating rather badly over the last ten to fifteen years and were closed for a time for both modernisation and conservation. In other words, doing what was necessary to bring the restaurant, shop and conference suite up to 21st Century standards whilst retaining as much of the 18th Century building as possible. The stables were built in 1755-1756 and the modernisation/conservation took place exactly 250 years later – 2005-2006!

Now, let us take a closer look at Thomas Chippendale. Kennedy[xxi] in her book offered some interesting insights about him. The first one is that in the past there was speculation that because of the proximity of Otley[14] (where Chippendale was born) and Harewood, that somehow Edwin Lascelles 'discovered' Chippendale. Nonsense say both the Harewood papers and one of Chippendale's biographers. Edwin Lascelles was simply ordering furniture, under the instructions of Robert Adam, from an elite firm in London, that of Chippendale and Haig in St Martin's Lane. The second insight was that during the time he was engaged at Harewood (1767 to 1778) he was also working on thirty other projects across the country. In Yorkshire, his work included Nostell Priory, Temple Newsam House, Burton Constable Hall, Newby Hall, Denton Hall and Goldsborough Hall. He is believed to have visited Harewood only twice, in September 1774 and February 1776[xxii].

Lancelot Capability Brown, England's most famous landscape gardener or architect, played a key part in the development of the Harewood Estate, which he worked on for nine years, beginning in 1772. Mauchline[xxiii] made an interesting comparison between the money Capability Brown was paid for his work and that of Thomas Chippendale. The money owed to Thomas Chippendale by June 1777 had risen to about £6850 in total for the furniture and furnishings of the house which was about £1000 more than Capability Brown's bill for landscaping of the park and pleasure grounds. However, Kennedy[xxiv] referred to Brown's bill being eventually about £16,000 which was three times the original estimate.

13.   Kirby Hall website. Kirby Hall, Northamptonshire, is one of England's greatest Elizabethan and 17th Century houses. The building of the house was begun by Sir Humphrey Stafford in about 1570.

14.   You may be interested to know that Otley in the 18th Century was already a market town of great antiquity, with a history going back to the Roman occupation. Sheltered beneath the towering, craggy shoulder of Otley Chevin, it was the hub of commercial activity for all the farms and feudal Estates in the area and the crafts associated with them. (Kennedy, 1982, p 42)

As another point of interest – what about the owner himself – Edwin Lascelles? What was he like to work for? Apparently he was quite prudent but how did this characteristic manifest itself? Well, for one thing his personal philosophy was to get the best as cheaply as possible. "He who wil do it most reasonably & at the same time well, shall alwaies be imployed by me".[xxv] Edwin Lascelles seemed to be a true Yorkshireman through and through! In *Harewood: A Guide* it was pointed out that "Edwin Lascelles was quite clearly a difficult customer with what is euphemistically known as a mind of his own. He was over forty when his father died and immediately set about realising the plans which must have been maturing in his mind for years"[xxvi]. Further, Kennedy[xxvii] stated that Edwin Lascelles was a "notoriously slow payer where hired professionals were concerned (though not with artisans)". An example that Kennedy[xxviii] gave was that Capability Brown's final Harewood bill was not paid until 1782, just one year before he died on 6th February 1783, aged 67.[15]

In terms of keeping costs down, whilst ensuring excellent quality, local sources were used for most of the basic materials. This included bricks, stone and gypsum for plaster, which came from land owned by Lascelles. Wood was the only material which had to be imported in any great quantity with the soft woods coming from the Baltic and the mahogany for the doors from the Lascelles estates in the West Indies.

Changes to Harewood House Over the Years

During the **Regency** period relatively little was altered within the House itself and some would say that in general the House was at a type of plateau. Yes, some Regency furnishings were added, but basically little changed since the time of Edwin Lascelles. The House was in no way declining or being poorly maintained, it was simply being used very effectively as the home of a gentleman. This was particularly true during the time of the 2nd Earl who was also Lord Lieutenant of the West Riding of Yorkshire. As Mauchline[xxix] pointed out, "Harewood House enabled him to maintain with ease and dignity the hospitality which was the duty and privilege of his Lieutenancy".

During the **Victorian** period, Harewood House was swept along with the many changes that were associated with Victorian England. In particular, by 1840, the Lascelles family were beginning to use the railway for their trips to

---

15. Capability Brown was taken ill and suddenly collapsed on returning home from a professional call on Lord Coventry in Piccadilly. A lifelong sufferer from asthma, he apparently fell down in a fit and died almost immediately at about 9pm in the evening. (Kennedy, 1982, p 56)

London, rather than travelling by coach and horses. The overall impact of the railway was significant. As Mauchline[xxx] pointed out, "isolation became merely nominal when a railway station was accessible in addition to a reasonably well-developed road system and visitors to Harewood had the choice of either the York or Leeds lines."

It was also during the Victorian period that Lady Louisa Thynne, the 3rd Countess, a forceful and energetic woman not dissimilar to Edwin Lascelles, commissioned Sir Charles Barry[16] to create more accommodation for the family. The work undertaken at that time resulted in the House we see today. His plans were submitted in 1842 and according to *Harewood: A Guide,*[xxxi] Barry's work "gave the house a third storey, swept away the classical portico on the south façade and added the massive Terrace which transformed the Georgian country house into something like an Italian palazzo."

In **20th Century** Harewood, according to Mauchline "the 5th Earl, Henry Lascelles (1846-1929), found himself on his father's death in 1892 faced with a dilemma he never personally solved: how to enjoy the expensive tastes of Edwardian society and how at the same time to live within his means so that that his Trustees were satisfied that the Estate was in no way diminished."[xxxii] The notion of keeping Trustees satisfied is a theme that continues until the current time, 2007, and I suspect that it always will. In other words, the key will always be ensuring that the books balance whilst maintaining all that Harewood House is and the treasures that it contains. Electricity was installed in Harewood House in 1901 but the cost of doing so meant that nothing else could be done to the House for a considerable period of time. In fact, it wasn't until the visit of King Edward VIII in 1908 that the Trustees granted the Earl an extra £700 towards the expense of the King's visit!

Lord Lascelles (the 5th Earl's eldest son who would become the 6th Earl), a very keen and extremely knowledgeable collector of fine art, fought in World War I with distinction. It was during the war years (1916 in London)

---

16. You might be interested to know that, according to Wikipedia, following the destruction by fire of the existing Houses of Parliament on 16 October 1834, Barry won the commission in 1836 to design the new Palace of Westminster. Work on site began with the laying of the foundation stone on 27 April 1840 by Barry's wife Sarah. The House of Lords was completed in 1847 and the House of Commons finished in 1852. In addition to the remodelling work he carried out at Harewood, he also designed the Trafalgar Square precinct, the HM Treasury building in Whitehall and Halifax Town Hall, West Yorkshire. He was knighted in 1852 on completion of the new Houses of Parliament.

that he briefly met his great uncle, the 2nd Marquess of Clanricarde. According to Mauchline[xxxiii], "on the Marquess's death shortly after this meeting, it was found that he had left the bulk of his fortune, estimated at £2,500,000, the derelict Portumna Castle in County Galway and his collection of Italian and Flemish paintings, to Lord Lascelles, a circumstance of the utmost significance in the history of Harewood House and a pleasing windfall to a man whose private income in 1910 had been reduced to £600." Apparently, why the Marquess left the bulk of his estate to his great-nephew rather than his nephew, is that he simply did not like his nephew, the then Lord Harewood.

After World War I, only essential repairs were carried out at Harewood because of the poor economic climate. The 5th Earl died in 1929 and in 1930, Viscount Lascelles who had been living at Goldsborough Hall, moved to Harewood as the 6th Earl. He and his wife, HRH Princess Mary (she became The Princess Royal in 1932), only daughter of King George V and Queen Mary, started to restore Harewood House – a task made much easier as a result of the Clanricarde inheritance.

The Earl asked the architect Sir Herbert Baker[17] for architectural advice – his plans were accepted and the House was carefully modernised with as little disruption as possible. The most important part of this work was the creation of a dressing room for Princess Mary.

According to Mauchline[xxxiv], Harewood House was a very distinguished residence by 1939 and was enriched by its collections of paintings, including the return of the Early English Watercolours which had originally been sold at Christies back in 1858. The reassembled collection included the 'Distant View of the South Front of Harewood House', which was dated 1798 and had been painted by Turner for Edward, Viscount Lascelles.

During World War II, Harewood House became a convalescent hospital, as it had in World War I, and as before the family retained only part of the House for themselves. During this time, it was reported that Sadler's Wells

---

17. According to Wikipedia, Sir Herbert Baker, (1862-1946), studied architecture in London but went to South Africa in 1892 where he was a dominant force for two decades – 1892 to 1912. Amongst his achievements: he and Edwin Lutyens were instrumental in designing New Delhi; he was commissioned by Cecil Rhodes in 1893 to remodel his house on the slopes of Table Mountain, Cape Town; he designed South Africa House in Trafalgar Square, London; he designed one of the grandstands at Lord's Cricket Ground in London, where he presented the MCC with the famous Father Time weather vane and he was also responsible for the rebuilding of the Bank of England.

Opera, who were appearing at the Grand Theatre in Leeds, came to perform 'The Marriage of Figaro' on an improvised stage at the South end of the Gallery. I am sure that Viscount Lascelles (George) would have approved – he was serving in the family regiment (Grenadier Guards) and after being wounded and taken prisoner, he spent his time in captivity in the study of music, especially opera. He would later become an international expert in the subject.

The 6th Earl died in 1947 before further work could be undertaken at Harewood, therefore the task of restoration passed to the 7th Earl, George Lascelles. Ongoing restoration continues to this day with major works being undertaken in the late 1980s and early 1990s. According to Mauchline[xxxv], "the impetus came from the rediscovery in a barn and in workshops in the Estate Yard, situated beyond Carr's Stables, of a treasure-trove of Chippendale's furniture and furnishings discarded by Barry during the decade of 'Victorianising' Harewood".

Initially I found it hard to understand how these treasures could have lain undiscovered for so many years and I thought it was a mystery that was unlikely ever to be solved. However, according to Lord Harewood, the mystery is actually easier to work out than I had at first thought! He explained that when the Victorians dismantled mirrors and other furniture, they tended to pack it away *very carefully* in cases. These were well known to the family but had never been explored properly until there was an attempt to put Adam's decoration back at the centre of the Harewood scheme. 'Carvers and Gilders' in London were the family's collaborators who looked at the Chippendale records and made a careful study of what they could find and what had to be restored, taken from the packing cases. So the real 'mystery' according to Lord Harewood, is that nothing was done either during his father's time, or until after he and the Countess had been at Harewood for some years. After that, Lord Harewood described it as "plain sailing, only rather expensive".

This section has concentrated primarily on the fabric and the architecture of Harewood House but what of the events that have taken place over the years and the people who have lived there?

The next sections contain a combination of factual information pertaining to events and activities within the Harewood Estate together with more personal stories taken mainly from newspaper articles. It is not intended to be a complete list of all events and visitors but will hopefully give you an overview of just some of the key moments from the last 200 years!

Famous Visitors

Harewood House has had many royal visitors, apart from being the home of Princess Mary and the 6th Earl of Harewood. The Tsar of Russia was entertained in 1816, and the Queen Dowager, Adelaide, wife of William IV, was a guest in 1830. The Duchess of Kent and the Princess Victoria visited Harewood House in 1835. King George V and Queen Mary, The Princess Royal's parents, paid many visits. Queen Elizabeth II, the Earl's cousin, came to Harewood during her Golden Jubilee tour on 11th July 2002. She had visited previously as a Princess and with the Duke of Edinburgh. Prince Charles has been to Harewood House several times, including a visit to take part in the opening ceremony of the Stupa built near the lake, in the same week that he married Camilla. In fact, that week in early April 2005 was a very busy one for Prince Charles. Not only did he take part in the opening of the Stupa, he also represented the Queen at the funeral of Pope John Paul II, on the 8th and got married on the 9th! (There is more information about the Stupa in Chapter Six, where in my discussions with David Lascelles, he outlines the history behind that particular project and the work involved in making his dream become a reality.)

In 2006 a number of famous people were spotted at Harewood House. It was mentioned in the Autumn/Winter edition of the *Harewood Card Newsletter* that Baroness Lola Young was there for the opening ceremony of the newly refurbished Courtyard; David Jason when filming 'Diamond Geezer' for YTV (using the Gallery as a look-alike for Buckingham Palace!); and other visitors that year included sports commentator Alan Hansen, actor Brian Blessed and singer Corinne Bailey Rae.

The above list of royal visitors to Harewood House, and celebrities, is, as you would expect, only a very small sample, since every year will see visits by celebrities and other important guests in both official and unofficial capacities.

Open to the Public

Most people, no doubt, believe that Harewood House has only been open to the public for a few years, as visiting stately homes seems to only have become widely popular over the last twenty to thirty years. How wrong people's perceptions can be! Wade[xxxvi] pointed out that the House became open to the public in 1950, although acknowledged that it was open prior to that, and Jewell[xxxvii] stated in 1819 that the House is "open to the public every Saturday, from eleven o'clock in the morning, until four o'clock in the afternoon; of which obliging permission, the nobility and gentry who frequent Harrogate, avail themselves much, the short distance forming a most agreeable excursion." As you will see from Olive Wild's scrapbook in Chapter Eight, the House was also opened in 1932 to raise money for charity, including funds for the Harewood Village Hall. The *Harewood News*[xxxviii] of August 1938 reported that Harewood House had been open to the public every Wednesday in June and July and that there were a total of 9,034 people visiting, which was an increase of 2,315 on 1937. Apparently bad weather in 1937 was partially to blame for the reduced numbers.

Exhibitions at Harewood House

In 1989, what was formerly the Sub Hall of Harewood House was refurbished specifically for use as an art gallery. It opened with an exhibition of contemporary works entitled "Images of Paradise" – the purpose of the exhibition was to focus attention on the world's rainforests. The works were on show for three months, following which they were auctioned at Harewood by the event sponsor, Christie's, in aid of Survival International. The Terrace Gallery has hosted paintings, sculpture, photography and film from an extraordinary range of contemporary artists ever since.

In 1995 Harewood developed its new watercolour rooms to showcase its own collections and to exhibit historic watercolours in the context for which they were originally intended. The first major exhibition in 1997 was the hugely successful 'Turner in the North' a collaboration with the Tate Gallery to celebrate the bicentenary of Turner's tour of the North of England which of course included Harewood House. The exhibition 'upstairs' was complemented by a commissioned suite of etchings by Norman Ackroyd entitled 'Tender is the North' which were shown in the Terrace Gallery.

Subsequently the Terrace Gallery has often housed a contemporary response to the historical, shown on the State Floor. The incredibly popular Chippendale exhibition of 2000 was initiated by Kate Whiteford, who installed the outline of a Chippendale sofa on an enormous scale in the landscape opposite the Terrace Gallery.

2002 brought George Stubbs' drawings for his important book 'The Anatomy of the Horse' which were notably contrasted by Mark Wallinger's contemporary work in the Terrace Gallery.

2004 saw the fruition of many years of work carried out in order to open up some of the areas 'below stairs' which had been used by servants and staff of the House since it was built. Originally intended as an 'open storage' project, the objects themselves dictated that the lives of maids, butlers, footmen, etc, would become the main theme. A special area was also created to look at the life of Princess Mary, wife of the 6th Earl.

Also in 2004, in conjunction with the Yorkshire Country House Partnership, the entire State Floor and Below Stairs became the platform for the 'Maids and Mistresses' exhibition. Each of the seven houses involved (Brodsworth Hall, Burton Constable Hall, Castle Howard, Lotherton Hall, Nostell Priory, Temple Newsam and Harewood House) interpreted the history of their women and produced an exhibition. As well as a display in the Watercolour Rooms which traced the lives of the ladies connected to the House, a trail around both floors looked at the women who lived and worked there.

By 2006, there was a desire to bring the historical closer to the current day. A film installation by Bill Viola the previous year had been immensely successful and the thoughts of the Harewood Trust about the use of the Watercolour Rooms were moving 'out of the box'. 'The Modern Show', staged in the Watercolour Rooms, brought together 50 works of British Modern Art from private collections, including pieces belonging to the Earl and Countess of Harewood and eight other collectors. Future plans involve the display of contemporary work on the State Floor and historical pieces in the Terrace Gallery.

Also in 2006, part of Harewood House remained open beyond the normal closing in November. In fact, the special exhibition 'Preparing for Christmas Below Stairs', did not close its doors until 17th December. As mentioned in the Autumn/Winter 2006/2007 edition of the *Harewood Card Newsletter*, "step back in time and enjoy a Victorian Yuletide experience, with Below Stairs dressed for Christmas 1890s style. The Steward's Room table will be laden with traditional Christmas puddings, pies and sweetmeats, and the Old Kitchen a hive of festive activity with food displays, presentations and daily baking demonstrations permeating the servants' corridors with mouth-watering spicy smells!"

Education at Harewood

Education is now at the heart of Harewood's work. Around 300 schools, colleges and universities from the Yorkshire Region and beyond visit the House and Grounds each year as well as many more people outside of formal learning. In 1986 Harewood became an educational charitable Trust and a progressive attitude to learning has been a feature of Harewood's development ever since. Harewood has a dedicated team of staff developing and delivering learning for schools, adults and community groups and in 2003 Harewood successfully completed a Heritage Lottery Funded programme for secondary schools. This innovative project has led on to 'Harewood Explored', a Heritage Lottery Funded project to get new audiences interested in British history. Harewood's high standard in the provision of education has resulted in a variety of awards including The Sandford Award in 2004 and Curiosity and Imagination: Roots and Wings in 2006.

Bird Garden and Adventure Playground

Harewood Bird Garden continues to be one of the best bird collections in the UK. Opened to the public in 1970 it is now home to around 325 birds consisting of 120 species from around the world. Over a third of the species present in the Bird Garden are classified from 'at risk' to 'endangered', in the wild. As an active member of the British and Irish Association of Zoos and Aquaria and the European Association of Zoos and Aquaria, many of the species participate in British, European or global breeding programmes and are extremely important in the fight to conserve their species.

The first Adventure Playground was opened in 1970 by footballer Jack Charlton and its successor in 1993 by Tony Dorigo.

Concerts

Harewood House has been the host of a tremendous range and type of concerts, including some 'pop' concerts, but mainly classical. However, 2006 marked the beginning of something very, very different, as it included the O2 Wireless Festival. The Festival was launched in 2005 in London, and Harewood was the venue chosen to host the Festival when it came to Leeds in 2006. Naturally, Harewood will continue to host classical concerts but it also looks like it is becoming a major venue for 'pop' concerts. The O2 Wireless Festival returned to Harewood in 2007 and other big concerts in 2006/2007 included James Blunt, Westlife, Simply Red and Jools Holland with special guest Lulu. I am not quite sure what Edwin Lascelles would have made of all of this, nor the present Earl when it comes to that, as I suspect that his taste in music is somewhat different, but one thing is certain, maintaining a vast Estate such as Harewood, and all of the treasures contained within the House, takes a considerable amount of money and since 'pop' concerts undoubtedly make a lot of money, perhaps the ends justify the means! I guess only time will tell.

Human Interest Stories During the 20th and 21st Centuries

The following is a selection, rather than a comprehensive record of events. Many were taken from newspaper articles that were unearthed following the death of Olive Wild. I am grateful to her nephew, Anthony Dring, for lending me the articles and books from Olive's collection.

1929

On 12th October, *The Yorkshire Weekly Post Illustrated* featured on its front cover the death of Lord Harewood, the 5th Earl. The title read: *Lord Harewood's Death: Yorkshire's Grief.* Some of the family pictures on the front page included 'the late Earl of Harewood, whose death has caused great grief in Yorkshire, where he was a very well-known figure'; Princess Mary and the former Viscount who became the Earl and Countess of Harewood; 'Florence, Lady Harewood, widow of the late Peer, has always been a keen supporter of all good works in the West Riding' and 'the King's grandson, the Hon. George Lascelles, now takes the title by which his father has been so well known, Viscount Lascelles'.

1935

On 6th May Silver Jubilee Celebrations for King George V and Queen Mary took place at Harewood Park. Within the Programme were the words that had been included in the telegram sent to the King and Queen from the residents of Harewood. "We, the inhabitants of Harewood and district, beg Their Majesties to accept our most loyal congratulations on the occasion of the Silver Jubilee, with the earnest hope that they may continue to have many happy years to reign over us. May we also express our sense of the great privilege we possess in that Harewood is the home of The Princess Royal."

1949

On 29th July *The Yorkshire Post* ran an article entitled, *Princess and Duke have home-made cakes for tea.* The article spoke about the tour of Yorkshire by Princess Elizabeth and the Duke of Edinburgh, including a house party at Harewood House. One of the two pictures in the article shows, amongst a number of other people, Princess Elizabeth, the Princess Royal, the Duke of Edinburgh and the Earl of Harewood taken outside Harewood House. The second picture shows Princess Elizabeth with a broad smile as she inspects members of the South Yorkshire branch of the Grenadier Guards Comrades' Association.

A few months later, on 29th September, the current Earl of Harewood married his first wife, Marion Stein, at St Mark's Church in London. You might be interested to know that the Bishop of Ripon officiated at the wedding and that one of those assisting him was none other than the Rev H H Griffith, the vicar of All Saints Church in Harewood from 1928 to 1974.

1953
The Yorkshire Post dated 28th December, showed on its front page a picture of the Princess Royal, Mrs Erwin Stein (the mother of the Countess), the Countess of Harewood and the Earl's second son, James Edward, after the baby's christening that took place at All Saints Church, Harewood. The article stated that the christening was far from a small family affair as friends and Estate workers crowded into the little Church for the ceremony.

1959
On the 2nd to 5th September, the Harewood Horse Trials European Championships took place at Harewood. Her Royal Highness The Princess Royal offered the following welcome at the beginning of the event programme. "As President this year of the British Horse Society I send a very warm welcome to all the Riders who are taking part in The Three Day Event at Harewood. I hope you will all enjoy your visit and have a very happy time. I extend a special welcome to all overseas visitors and those from foreign countries who have come such a long way to Yorkshire to take part in the greatest horse event in Europe this year." It was simply signed, Mary.

1962
On 17th March the Combined Charities Fashion Show took place at Harewood House. The event was in aid of the British Red Cross Society, Leeds Multiple Sclerosis Society, Spring Houses Home for Children and the Leeds Musical Festival. The committee to the event made the following comments at the beginning of the event brochure: "The Committee are grateful to HRH The Princess Royal and to Lord and Lady Harewood for kindly permitting this event to take place in Harewood House. They also desire to express their thanks to Hardy Amies and to Madame Rose Vernier for kindly giving their services in presenting their collections."

1967
On 13th January *Time* magazine ran an article entitled, 'The Liabilities of Being a Lord'. In this article the magazine pointed out how very difficult it

is for a member of the extended Royal Family, because of the Royal Marriages Act of 1772, to remarry once divorced, and especially to someone who themselves is also divorced. The article pointed out the various options Lord Harewood had in terms of getting remarried but at that time, was only able to speculate as to what he would actually do. Lord Harewood made up his mind and married Patricia Tuckwell on 31st July 1967 in New Canaan, Connecticut, in the United States.

1970

In May 1970 *The Leeds Graphic* carried an extensive article, including a variety of photographs, pertaining to the opening of the Bird Garden at Harewood House. In addition, in the introduction to the May edition, there is a great picture of Mark Lascelles and the Countess of Harewood. The caption under the picture reads: "Six year old Master Mark Lascelles looks somewhat apprehensive as this friendly macaw perches on his shoulder to the evident amusement of his mother, the Countess of Harewood." He certainly did look rather worried!

1978

Book published – *50 Years Gardening at Harewood* by Geoffrey Hall. In the Foreword to the book the Earl stated that Geoff Hall's family had been associated with Harewood and its gardens for two generations. It is a fascinating book with many insights into both the gardens of Harewood and also to Princess Mary who was an extremely keen and knowledgeable gardener.

1981

A newspaper article, which unfortunately, was not able to be identified because little of the original article remains, indicated that 1981 was a reflective time for Lord Harewood. In this article the Earl reflected on his life to date, which was prompted by the publication of his autobiography in the same year – *The Tongs and the Bones*. The article was basically a very quick overview of his extremely well written and fascinating book. In the part of the article that remained intact, the Earl mentioned countless happy memories of his childhood, his mother, the Princess Royal, his grandparents, time spent at Harewood House and so on. However, the article also mentioned the great sadness the Earl felt after losing the friendship of Benjamin Britten as a result of his divorce and deciding to resign from his job as artistic director of the Edinburgh Festival for the same reason. Furthermore, the Earl spoke very openly about undergoing psychoanalysis for two years back in the 1960s, not because he felt that he was going 'mad' but as a way of clearing his mind – in the words of the Earl, "a great clarifier which threw light on a difficult situation".

1986

The Country Landowners Association Game Fair came to Harewood for the first time in the Summer of 1986. The Foreword in the programme was written by Lord Harewood and in it he stated: "It is a great pleasure to welcome everyone connected with the Game Fair to Harewood – visitors, participants and organisers. This is the first time it has been here and my wife and I hope we can provide the kind of hospitality for which Yorkshire is renowned, the weather which the season suggests, the surroundings the Game Fair deserves, and the kind of event everyone will enjoy."

1990

In a publication called *Select: Yorkshire Ridings Edition*, there was a fascinating article written about the restoration work that Lord and Lady Harewood were undertaking at Harewood House. The article, written by Judith Halliday, began with the following words: "Lady Harewood is not your everyday countess. For a start, she is an enthusiastic Leeds United supporter with few nice words to say about the Argentinians after the damp squib of a World Cup final, a tournament which kept her husband and herself fully engrossed for the best part of a month. But, as the author found out when she visited them at their beautiful West Yorkshire home, they have a rather more pressing concern than the ups and downs of Maradona and company. Their long-term plan is to restore Harewood House to its former glory, a project costing millions, and with meticulous planning necessary to keep their own 'spectators' happy."

1994

On 14 April the *Harrogate Advertiser* ran an article entitled *Planting the seed of regeneration*. The newspaper's reporter Sarah-Jane Leydon took a walk with Harewood House's head gardener Michael Walker in order to explore some of the changes that were taking place. According to the article, the family called the 'under construction' terraced gardens 'a battlefield'. Although the pictures accompanying the article did give the impression that there was still a great deal of work yet to do, by July the gardens were ready for the grand re-opening. In fact, they were officially completed on 7th July, exactly 150 years to the day since the garden was originally completed to an Italianate plan by Sir Charles Barry, the designer of the Houses of Parliament.

1998

The following was taken from a newspaper article dated 24th April. "More than 200 staff members joined Lord and Lady Harewood this week in a photograph which brought back memories from Harewood House's past. The Earl and Countess of Harewood, Viscount and Viscountess Lascelles and

Hon Mark and Andrea Lascelles and their children, sat patiently in front of the House steps on Monday afternoon as Bradford-based photographer Ian Beesley recreated photographs from 1930 and 1950. It is believed Lord Harewood is the only person to have appeared in all three pictures – the first as a seven year old sitting between his parents, the 6th Earl and Princess Mary. The photograph taken this week was part of Harewood's celebration of Photo 98, the Year of Photography and Electronic Image and was on the initiative of David, Viscount Lascelles who is chairman of Photo 98. Although duties and responsibilities have changed greatly at Harewood since the 1930s, remarkably, there was still almost exactly the same number of staff from the Estate and the Trust who posed for the 1998 version." The pictures taken were placed on display at the House as part of its exhibition for Photo 98.

2002
On 11th July Her Majesty the Queen's Golden Jubilee Visit Celebration took place at Harewood. Within the Programme for this great event the Earl made the following comments. "It is both a delight and privilege to be welcoming Her Majesty the Queen to Harewood in this Golden Jubilee Year. We have not many hours in which to celebrate with her the diversity and strengths of this wonderful county of West Yorkshire, but those of us fortunate enough to live here will do our best to make the most of the window we have been given onto a crowded programme."

"I remember the Queen visiting the West Riding in 1949, when she was still Princess Elizabeth: she was at Harewood again in 1958 for the centenary Leeds Festival and in 1965 for my mother's funeral. July 11th will we hope be a memorable day in a memorable year, for the Queen as well as for all of us here at Harewood, indeed for all West Yorkshire, and we might echo the Scottish chant, raised originally in a very different context: 'Will ye no' come back again: better loued ye canna be.'"

You might find it interesting to note that tucked safely within the Programme was Olive Wild's personal invitation to attend the Jubilee Festival Parade and Garden Party at Harewood House.

During the Queen's Golden Jubilee tour of the UK the BBC's Arts and Media Correspondent, Nick Higham, followed the Queen on her tour. His 11th dispatch, on 11th July, began with: "They know how to push the boat out in Yorkshire. The West Riding, as it used to be called, has laid on one of the most flamboyant days in the Queen's Jubilee tour of the UK: a shrewd mix of popular culture and pomp, public spectacle and family reunion – the whole shot through with constant reminders of what Yorkshire has given the world."

2005

The Summer issue of *The Harewood Times* led with an article about HRH The Prince of Wales and his visit to Harewood. The first paragraph of the article stated: "On Tuesday, 5th April, HRH The Prince of Wales attended the consecration ceremony of the Harewood Stupa in the Himalayan Garden. The Stupa had been constructed during 2004 by local Yorkshire craftsmen, assisted by monks from Bhutan and under the supervision of master Stupa builder Lama Sonam Chophel. Prince Charles kindly accepted an invitation from Lord Lascelles to visit Harewood for this special occasion." As mentioned earlier, on Saturday of this same week Prince Charles married Camilla Parker-Bowles in Windsor.

In the same issue of *The Harewood Times*, reference was also made to the Harewood Castle Conservation Project, "since the last newsletter, the repair works have continued to proceed smoothly and the contract is now entering the final stages, with 85% completed, and only consolidation to the interior wall faces to the North West Tower and Kitchen Range remaining." The Project was completed later in 2005.

In addition, in 2005 Harewood House was awarded the title of 'most popular visitor attraction in Yorkshire'.

2007

The *Yorkshire Evening Post* on 1st February contained an article entitled *Slave to the Rhythm* in which it mentioned a number of activities that will take place to mark the 200 years since the end of slavery. One of the activities is Carnival Messiah that will be taking place on the grounds of Harewood during September.

The Ice House, designed by John Carr and built in 1761 to store ice for use in the kitchen, has been restored and opened to the public.

2007 has seen the return of the O2 Wireless Festival in the Summer and the introduction of Yorkshire's only planetarium. The Harewood House website described the planetarium as:

> "Yorkshire's first planetarium, a pair of linked geodesic domes will house two unique visual experiences. Step inside the Starchamber and explore the night sky. Be led around the constellations and the planets that can be seen from Yorkshire every night revealed in all its breathtaking glory, undimmed by light pollution. From the sky at night follow the Bay tree walk into the Hubble Space Dome,

brings us images directly from the Hubble Telescope."

The CLA Game Fair was due to take place in the grounds of the Harewood Estate from 27th–29th July. Unfortunately, because of the adverse weather conditions which caused the grounds to become waterlogged, the Game Fair was cancelled for the first time in its 49 year history.

End Notes

i   Edmund Bogg, *A Thousand Miles in Wharfedale*, (printed from the internet on 2nd March 2006) (1892), p 8.
ii   Ibid, pp 4 and 5.
iii   Carol Kennedy, *Harewood: The Life and Times of an English Country House* (1982), p 32.
iv   Harewood House Trust, *Harewood: A Guide*, p 5.
v   Kennedy, op cit, p 32.
vi   Ibid, p 59.
vii   Harewood House Trust, op cit, p 55.
viii   Simon Smith, *Slavery, Family and Gentry Capitalism in the British Atlantic: The World of the Lascelles, 1648-1834* (2006), p 3.
ix   BBC website, *Slavery and Harewood House*, c 2007, p 1.
x   Smith, op cit, p 73.
xi   BBC website, op cit, p 1.
xii   Smith, op cit, pp 86 and 87.
xiii   BBC website, op cit, p 1.
xiv   Smith, op cit, pp 88 and 89.
xv   Ibid, p 90.
xvi   BBC website, op cit, p 1.
xvii   Bogg, op cit, p 5.
xviii   Kennedy, op cit, p 24.
xix   Derek Linstrum, *West Yorkshire Architects and Architecture* (1978), pp 73 and 74.
xx   Ibid, p 31.
xxi   Kennedy, op cit, p 43.
xxii   Ibid, p 48.
xxiii   Mary Mauchline, *Harewood House*, p 86.
xxiv   Kennedy, op cit, p 55.
xxv   Mauchline, op cit, p 21.
xxvi   Harewood House Trust, op cit, p 5.
xxvii   Kennedy, op cit, p 42.
xxviii Ibid, p 56.
xxix   Mauchline, op cit, p 120.
xxx   Ibid, p 122.
xxxi   Harewood House Trust, op cit, p 8.
xxxii   Mauchline, op cit, p 143.
xxxiii Ibid, p 145.
xxxiv   Ibid, p 151.
xxxv   Ibid, p 157.
xxxvi   Ron Wade, *Vat Sal Be Sal* (1982), p 62.
xxxvii John Jewell, *The Tourist's Companion of the History and Antiquities of Harewood* (1819), p 7.
xxxviii Harewood House, *Harewood News*, August 1938

CHAPTER SIX
Discussions with
The Earl and The Viscount

The Harewood Family Flag

Introduction

My meeting with the 7th Earl, Lord Harewood, took place on Tuesday, 19th December, and with the Viscount, David Lascelles, on Thursday, 30th November, 2006.

As one would expect, there was common ground between the two generations in terms of some of their views, but in many other ways, the discussions could not have been more different. For a start, my meeting with David Lascelles took place in his office in the House which could be described as relatively small but functional and certainly very bright, with two windows overlooking the grounds. The general 'feel' of the interview was quite 'up-beat' and forward looking. By contrast, the meeting with the Earl took place in his very comfortable and cosy private study. This study, which he shares with the Countess, is high in the House and overlooks the lake. It has the feel of a Victorian parlour with its ticking clock, open fire, books everywhere and general 'clutter' that gave the room a lovely lived-in feel. The general 'feel' of the meeting with the Earl was that of reflection and contemplation. Both meetings were extremely enjoyable and informative and I feel very privileged and grateful for these two very busy men to have given me so much of their valuable time and for being so open with their answers to the questions I posed.

The information presented below represents the essence of the discussions I had with the Earl and David Lascelles. In other words, it is not a complete word-for-word transcript.

Discussion with Lord Harewood

Lord Harewood, what do you consider to be the key events in your life over the past ten years or so?

The first key event was when I gave control of the house to my son David. To begin with, it was a great surprise to me when I realised that I no longer owned anything by way of land and so on. My father died when I was about 24 and ever since then I have owned various tracts of this part of Yorkshire. It dawned on me that I no longer did. On the other hand, it has been a wonderful take-over, he (David) is very involved, he is positive and I find that very good and I don't have any real regrets at all. David and I talk a lot about what is going on, which is very useful from my point of view. We don't discuss things on the basis of a 'yes' or 'no', black or white, – we talk about them rather than about the decisions that have to be made, and usually I think that his decisions are pretty good.

He has done something that was very positive with the development at Stank of what was the farm – very grand, when you look at those buildings which are now occupied by businesses, large or small. I think that has made a very successful business, which was entirely down to him, not me. Actually, my wife suggested it (the development of the farm) after she had seen something comparable in another part of Yorkshire. She was rather played down by our then Agent but within a year when David took over, she mentioned it to him and he and Christopher Ussher (the Resident Agent) immediately adopted the idea. And the rest, as they say, is history.

I would be interested in hearing your views with reference to the project to conserve Harewood Castle. (I found his views fascinating in that it was not what I expected!)

Well, I take the view that if something is a ruin it is a ruin and it gradually finds its own place, its own state. You don't work to make a ruin something else, unless you decide to, but that is a different decision and it is no longer a ruin. I think that to have spent a lot of money on the Castle was frankly ridiculous in that I think it is money that would have been better spent elsewhere. Fortunately, at least half of the money spent on the Castle was provided by English Heritage. But, on the whole, I did not find the money well spent.

When I questioned him further, he went on to say that gaining access to the Castle was going to be extremely difficult and therefore the project was very unlikely ever to pay. Further, I asked him if it was, in the end, a decision he supported even though he did not agree with it. Yes, was his very clear answer.

What are the two or three fondest memories you have of Harewood House?

This is my home, I have lived here since I was seven, since 1930 when my parents came to live here. I already knew the House as I came here as a little boy. I came with my brother to stay here when I was about five or six. He was very little and I was allowed to go down to lunch with my grandparents which I thought was very grand, appropriate and agreeable. I saw a programme on television the other night which reminded me of my time here as a little boy when I took a bath in front of a fire in an old hip bath. It was perfectly nice except that you got cold when you got out! I thought at the time that my grandparents were quite old fashioned because we had baths, not hip baths, at Goldsborough Hall, where I lived with my parents.

I have been on walks here from a very early age when I was four, five or six, round the grounds here. The House is a major part of my life and of course it has always been a background in my life. When I was a very little boy we came here and I went to school and school was away and it was a live-in school, so for more than half the year I wasn't here. After, when I was older, in the war, I was in the Army and I was only here when on leave. In the war I was abroad and I was a Prisoner of War by the end of the war. It wasn't until I came back, that I lived here all the time. But it has always been the biggest part of the background of my life. In a way one's home however important it is to you, it is almost certainly not more than a background in one's life because you go out and do something else. But it was still the most important part of the background of my life, obviously much more now as I don't go away very much. I am 83 as we talk. We go to London occasionally, but we tend to cancel more than we go. I am very happy sitting here looking out at the changes that happen out there in the grounds. (JM – I am not surprised).

I know from what I have heard, what I have read, and through things you have written that music has also played a very significant role in your life and that in many respects you are a world expert in various aspects of music. Do you have any favourite stories about that, any people you have met …?

Not really, I have known a lot of musicians better or less well. Ever since I was a Prisoner of War, I have read a great deal about music. Fortunately, we had a lot of books in the two camps I was in. Therefore, I found out a great deal from book reading and then I worked in music when I came out. I started a magazine and ran it and I went constantly to performances. I ran festivals, worked in opera companies and I got to know a great deal about the inside middle men of music, I have always been a middle man – putting performances together. I am not a practising musician, unfortunately. I have worked for orchestras and opera companies and festivals, and that was very interesting because of course they were quite different, substantially different. For example, in festivals you not only do operatic work, cause operatic work to happen, but you cause symphony concerts and chamber concerts to happen as well and I enjoyed that very much and it taught me a great deal. My wife and I have been married for 39 years and for 38 of those years, I think, we have run concerts here throughout the winter – chamber concerts. The work I did for the Edinburgh Festival, and before that the Leeds Festival, was very much a preparatory work for the concerts we run here. I have been very lucky, I have spent most of my life working for and in the thing that has given me the most pleasure – music. It is not everyone who is as fortunate as I have been – to work in something you enjoy most and something that has given you the most satisfaction.

Who do you see as your successor, or successors, in the things you used to do in music or have you already passed much of your work to other people?

Other people do the jobs I used to do. If we take Opera North, which I helped to found, I am still on the Board and I talk a great deal to the people who work in it and I have an element of influence. On the other hand, as you get old, you ought to influence practical concerns, things you have worked at in the past, like an opera company or symphony orchestra, but one ought to forego the day to day influence you once had. I can't tell people (I can but I don't) what they should do, who they should get. I can criticise the outer aspects of one or two opera companies I have worked with, things like that, but you can't expect to, as it were, run those things any more. I always say to them, look I know I am quite useful to discuss repertory for instance, based on my experience of the past. You can't expect to have day-by-day influence or if you do you are mistaken. I enjoy talking to the people who run opera companies here and in London. I talk to them about their work and what their plans are and I enjoy that very much.

Why opera? Why not ballet? Why did you decide opera?

I liked the noise of the singers, the sound they make, first of all on gramophone records and then in real life and that's been an area of expertise for all my life. I think it's the most complicated and in a certain way it is the most interesting form of performance that I know of, or anybody else knows of. I would argue that position as a matter of principal for as long as you like. It involves more things than other forms of performance and it gives me immense satisfaction. I find it amazing that in ballet people don't break into song, very occasionally they do, but not very often, I think ballet is very agreeable but its not for me, whereas opera is, it involves me, ballet doesn't. I like ballet but I like it less than the straight theatre which I like very much. Of course when I was in any of the festivals I ran, it involved straight theatre as well as opera. Nowadays at my advanced age, any expedition, even going to Leeds is an expedition, even though someone else drives. It is an expedition in the sense that it disrupts your timescale and almost certainly happens at a time when you would rather be doing something else – like eating – and you come back at a time when it is already late to go to bed, so we go into Leeds but not very often for a perform-ance, which is regrettable but that's how it goes. When we go to London it is a bigger displacement.

If we look to the future, to the Harewood 'experience', if you want to call it that, what do you see changing over the next few years to make the experi-ence even more desirable?

I don't think I would use the word "changing", I'd use the word "evolving". I think that things evolve and seem to exist for different evolved purposes, different from the ones in the past. My ancestors bought and lived in this House as a very private thing, I have no doubt that Edwin built this House partly to impress his peers, his friends, but that was a normal thing to do, people did that in those days. People may still do that but I don't think that has much to do with this place. I think that it has a different function in life. I think that it no longer is entirely for this family to live in it and take advantage of its various agreeableness, comforts, excitements, possibilities, and so on. I think the House and Estate can offer quite a lot to people outside and I think that is something that David is good at and I think he thinks about that sort of thing much more than I did. The House, the Estate, can offer people who want to go round it purely for the agreeable experience of seeing it, seeing how the luckier half lives, or lived, but I think it also has other possibilities of teaching, teaching is a rather limiting word, but of showing people various things about life, possibilities, outlooks and so on, which are worthwhile. I think David is very much into that and it is one of the things that Harewood can do and I think that it is probably starting to do, has been starting to do, more than when I was running it and I think that is very good. I like looking at the developments here from a comfortable distance, I think it is quite exciting. David has a lot of thoughts about what can be put on here, sometimes in terms of perform- ance. For example, there were two tremendous rock concerts here last Summer. We were going to go away but didn't go away, all we did was put in ear plugs instead!! It was supposed to stop at 10.30pm. Anyway, there was a lot of pounding going on. I think it is quite nice, I didn't want to be there but I think it was quite nice.

Next year David is going to do Carnival Messiah which was started in Leeds some years ago. He is going to do that and it is a very big enterprise next year which I think is quite exciting. It is exciting because it is worthwhile in itself because it is a tie with the immigrant population of Leeds, the black people in Leeds, many of whom were born here but many have come from the West Indies and we used to have a big West Indian interest in that we had property in Jamaica and Barbados. I was the last person, I sold what my father had left me, about 30 years ago. I used to like the West Indies very much and this is a kind of gesture to do with the abolition of slavery, the 200th anniversary, which is next year, this Carnival Messiah and I think that's all interesting and worthwhile and I'd really like him to come up with many other things over the years.

Do you regard yourself as a person who is constantly looking towards the future or do you tend to look back on the past?

I am interested in the past, I like to look at the things from the past because that is interesting and to disregard them is foolish but I have always looked to the future. If you run festivals or opera you must look to the future, at least you are no good at it if you don't and I actually wasn't bad at it, so I hope I am always looking towards the future.

I remember that after my mother died, which was a very long time ago – over

40 years – 1965 – Neville Ussher who had been running the Estate as my Agent for many years, said something like "we ought to make the house work a little bit for its own upkeep, as well as what we put into it". I was very lucky that I had one of my closest friends running the Estate. We met first of all as ADCs in Canada.

What are your views in terms of the relationship between the Harewood Estate, the House and the village itself?

It is a complicated question because the prosperity, if that's the right word, of the village is partly dependent on what we make possible through the House, the park and everything else. I think the wellbeing of people living in the village is an important thing and always has been, for my family before, for me more recently and for David now, but I think it is difficult to make an absolutely simple, direct, relationship between the two. Funny things occur to me, I remember when they first told us they were going to put traffic lights in the village and we thought it was an idiotic idea. But, we couldn't stop them and it was right that we didn't. Today, we are absolutely dependent on them to get in and out of the Estate, so that's an ordinary piece of evolution. I think that my family used to own all of the village and I have sold a lot because to begin with I needed the money, and secondly I thought it could stand on its own. I think we always take account of the needs of the village when we make decisions here, I think we would always take that into account – I certainly did, my father certainly did and I think David certainly would. What will happen in the future, I have no idea, but I would guess and hope that that is maintained as a point of view.

What are your views on All Saints Church?

Well I hope it goes on. Quite a lot of money has been put into it recently since it became a redundant church, of course it has different patronage, and that's good because it is in much better order with the tombs and such re-sited and so on. I think it will go on in that way, it is still used on high days if not all holidays. You can't fill it now unless you have a carol service or something.

What do you see as the relationship between the Estate itself and the Trust?

I think they are dependent on each other. I think that the Estate is in many ways flourishing and the Trust would have a harder job, if it were not for the Estate, and maybe vice-versa. I think the Estate might find it very difficult to compete with all the things that the Trust is supposed to do and takes responsibility for.

How often do you correspond with your cousin Queen Elizabeth, do you correspond with her very often?

Well, really only when there are events that would concern her. There was a big garden party here and she came of course to that, which was actually rather fun. Very occasionally there is something at Windsor or Buckingham Palace or one of the great churches in London which concern us but not very often. For instance, once there was a big dinner party at Windsor, huge number of people, many of whom I didn't know, and I wrote and said thank you because that's what you do when you dine with someone, which is effectively what we were doing. Not on a day-to-day basis at all, but she sends us a Christmas card.

I will tell you something you possibly don't know. The Queen Mother used to address the envelopes herself – to her family. The Queen doesn't. The Queen on the other hand, if you write on a mutual concern, she writes back and doesn't get someone else to do it – to people like cousins, like me.

I understand that you knew Maria Callas – can you tell me something about her?

I probably knew her better than anyone in England. When she had retired but not officially retired, the BBC wanted to do some broadcast with her and she asked for me as the person who knew her best and respected her most. We went to Paris to interview her for the BBC programme. I saw her regularly since first meeting her in 1947. Our first meeting was a pure accident, when she made her debut in Italy, in Verona. There was a dinner party given by the mayor, and I sat next to her at dinner and after the dinner we talked a great deal. After that I used to see her very frequently.

Who do you see as her successor?

She was absolutely unique – not only a splendid performer of music, but she had an imagination and an instinct which was just above other people's. There are very good singers but nobody as good as that.

In addition to Maria Callas, are there any others who you hold in such high esteem?

I knew a lot of the singers of that period very well – Boris Christov for instance I knew well. He was a great singer. Hans Hotter I knew quite well. I got him his ticket for the final of the world cup in 1966 – he was of course naturally very pro German – but he never paid for it! He has sung here and that sort of thing. A quite good book was published about him in English and I heard that

Covent Garden had said that they would not give a little lunch party to launch it, so I did it in the Coliseum instead and he was very pleased.

You mentioned the World Cup. Are you still actively involved with Leeds United Football Club?

I am. I still go every other Saturday, I am going this Saturday – I didn't go last Saturday because they were at Ipswich. It seems to me we were unlucky not to do well in that, but we lost and we are one above bottom. It's a bad place to be. On the other hand, if you are only a fair-weather supporter, you are not a supporter at all, so we go.

What will you be doing in the Springtime? What do you look forward to?

In the Spring? Well of course the coming of the Spring is great excitement with the flowers and shrubs coming. I think you become more conscious of the beauties of nature and therefore of the seasons as you get older. I like Autumn, I like all the seasons, but I love Spring. It seems to me that not to do so is unnatural.

What do you mean by that?

If you don't react to the natural beauties of Spring, then you have lost a valuable perception, and I do.

Do you have a favourite walk?

Well, I have asthma and if I go out and walk only a short distance I gasp a lot so we don't really do walks any more – we have a golf buggy for the Spring and Summer and we go in that, round the lake.

Discussion with Lord Lascelles (or David Lascelles as he prefers to be addressed)

The discussion began by David asking me to give him some background as to why I was writing the book. I mentioned my reasons which included the fact that the last new book about Harewood was published in 1982, although one book originally published in 1974 was revised and reprinted in 1992. In other words, I felt that it was time to bring the history of Harewood up to date, but I also wanted to include the village and general area, not just Harewood House.

I think what you say is very interesting in relation to the various histories of Harewood and certainly what I have felt increasingly is that the history of Harewood has very much been based around the history of Harewood House and the people who lived in it. But, as you mentioned, the history of Harewood has a much wider history, including the fact that it can be traced back to the Bronze Age.

How Henry Lascelles made his money in the West Indies is an important part of Harewood's history. It is interesting that detailed research on this has only recently been carried out by researchers from the University of York, although the material has been in existence for over 200 years. The book, based on the research findings, is a very academic book, but he (the author Dr Simon Smith) *has built up a pretty comprehensive picture of that period and how the family in a very short period of time went from being fairly small scale North Yorkshire landowners, to one of the richest families in the country. Their fortune was made on the back of the sugar trade, slave trade and so on. What I found fascinating was how Henry in particular seemed to be doing much the same as many others but it seemed that he was smarter, a better businessman, whatever the morality of what the business was, which nowadays of course we see as being appalling. At the time, those qualms didn't exist and he was just a better businessman than most of the rest of them in the way he went about his business and the way he tied different aspects of the business together and made sure he controlled every aspect of it – vertical integration as it is now known – I don't think anybody called it that then but that is what he was doing, no doubt about it.*

Slight sidetrack, but all those histories – I always say history should be a plural because history is somebody's version of events taken from a particular slant with a particular set of interests, sometimes a particular axe to grind, all sorts of things.

One of the things I am particularly interested in, and would like your perspective on, is how the Estate and the Trust work together.

They are two separate organisations. Harewood House Trust was set up in 1986 and ran under one management till Terry Suthers was appointed in the early 1990s as head of the Trust. Prior to his appointment there had always traditionally been a land agent or controller or whatever you want to call it, who ran the Harewood Estate and everything in it but no one heading the Trust. It seemed to me at the time we made that appointment that we had two organisations which should be headed up by two different people. On the one hand, Harewood House Trust is an educational charity and you have to be very scrupulous about how a charity is run, how its finances are run, particularly a charity set up by a family to look after a House like this – there can be absolutely no reservation of benefit, the family cannot benefit in any way from the Trust's charitable status and the scrutiny is pretty rigorous.

It was at that time that we thought that the two organisations needed separate skills and sets of knowledge in order to run them. To run the House as a successful visitor attraction (at that time it was a moderately successful visitor attraction, not hugely successful it must be said, with dwindling numbers and so on) required different skills than those needed to run a country estate, e.g. to know about the grazing rights and run forestry schemes and so on. It would be very unlikely for one person to encompass all those skills. So, in order to kind of solidify, if you like, the clear identity between the family business, the Harewood Estate, and Harewood House Trust, educational charitable Trust, opening the House and making the House and grounds and contents available to the public for their benefit, you need two separate management structures which had never existed at Harewood before. It has been by and large very successful.

The Trust has gone from strength to strength, visitor numbers have gone up, public profile has gone up, and I think in the area there is a much stronger sense of identity. Further, we have been able to attract public funding, and have won awards for our educational programme and so on.

The Estate on the other hand, not having to support the House or look after it, has been able to become quite a successful stand-alone business – largely a property company, managing assets. Quite a number of the houses in the village are still owned by the Estate, farm buildings have been converted into offices, farmhouses have been done up and rented out etc. So it is becoming a very successful, small to medium sized, property business. The Estate and the Trust have existed quite well in parallel.

At times there is a gap between the two organisations but in the end it is all working to the same end. I mean Harewood is one entity, the Trust just happens to occupy the land in the bulls eye, the middle of the target and the Estate sits around, but you can't separate out the two, not really.

Can I offer you a very practical example of where there could be a gap between the two – the fireworks at the end of major concerts. The fireworks naturally attract people but from the Estate's point of view, the fireworks frighten the life out of the wildlife, especially the deer who run into the fences. Therefore it must be difficult at times to attempt to attract more people here without potentially harming the Estate and that's tricky.

Absolutely, exactly. It is tricky and there is no single answer to that, its just a case-by-case answer and you've got to really weigh up everything that happens here as to what the benefits are and what the downsides might be.

On that same theme, how do you see the Harewood 'experience' developing over the next four or five years, or however many years you can look out to?

Well I think the offering here is pretty good. The vast majority of people who come here of course don't come into the House or don't go to the 'below stairs' exhibition. They come for a walk or a picnic or just to play on the adventure playground or whatever. I think that without being complacent about it, the mix of activities here is by and large right. What we have never done is to try to chase the new sensation, the new ride. We made a very conscious decision about that a long time ago, really when we appointed Terry Suthers, to better present the huge range of assets that Harewood has got, and make people feel more welcome when they come to see them. In a nutshell that's what we do, rather than trying to reinvent Harewood as a fantastic theme park with fairground rides or wild animals or whatever.

However, we have tried, and will continue to try, to find special interest things which have been pretty significant in terms of our audience figures. For example, the Turner exhibition a few years ago which was hugely popular, or at the other end of the spectrum, the 'Walking with Dinosaurs' show for kids a few years ago. These are examples of blockbuster shows that clearly are very popular for different reasons. In 2007 for example we are opening, on a one year trial basis, what I think will be Yorkshire's first planetarium and I think there will be a lot of interest in that. We shall see, I am naturally cautious about these things. The planetarium might very well turn out to be another one of those blockbusters. So we will continue to introduce and look for, things which are appropriate but we are not looking to radically change the nature of what goes on here.

In terms of access to certain parts of the Estate, I have always wondered why there isn't a circular walk around the lake.

I believe that there is pretty good access generally speaking in the Estate, both within the Trust land and the public footpaths which criss-cross the Estate. There are some areas which are not accessible – as you say, the far side of the lake is one of the relatively few bits of the Estate that can't be reached. I think it is important to have areas that are relatively unvisited for conservation purposes and actually we have quite an exceptional range of birds and other animals here on the Harewood Estate. Some of that has been consciously done, for example, the introduction of the red kites, and on a smaller scale we introduced barn owl breeding on the North Park. We have been very successful in looking after the countryside, having a variety of habitats, woodland, wetland, grass parks and so on. The management of the North Park has changed radically in the last few years. We have taken fences down and added others in order to turn the area into a deer park. As a result of doing so, the whole ecology of the area has changed. We are trying to keep a balance between accessibility and non-accessibility. There have been lots of other debates, for example the walled garden – there is a part that you can visit at the end of the lake walk and the other half which the public footpath runs along the edge. There have been discussions at all sorts of different times whether there could be something there, for example, a garden centre, or whatever, but then you have the issues regarding access.

If we go onto the question about the most memorable things for you, including the Stupa, I am interested in how that came about.

Certainly in recent years that is one of the most memorable things and I am completely responsible for it, or to blame for it, however you want to put it!

I have a longstanding interest in that part of the world, having travelled a lot in that area, and in the late 70s I made a series of documentary films in India, Nepal and so on, about Tibetans in exile. At that point it was impossible to get into Tibet at all so we visited Dharamsala in North India where the Dalai Lama is, Tibetan settlements in Nepal and Ladakh on the borders between Kashmir and Tibet. This is an area which is geographically and socially most likely old Tibet. Very much the same sort of structure, the monastery on the hill, village cluttered round the foot of the hill and so on. We made a series of films there, recently re-released, and so I have had a longstanding interest in that part of the world. Stupas are everywhere there, tops of mountain passes, village centres, courtyards, monasteries. They are a symbol of the Buddhist faith which is universal across the Himalayas, but also a very accessible manifestation of it, somewhere people go, not to pray necessarily but to go and walk round, a normal thing to do with a Stupa is to walk round it. It was for a very long time one of those 'what if', 'wouldn't it be nice if' sort of thoughts about having one here.

In 2002 I visited Bhutan for the first time and the idea really re-surfaced again. I was thinking that there must be someone here who could build one for us, as people here do this sort of thing all the time. You have to keep in mind that building a Stupa is quite a specific skill, as it is made to very precise specifications and dimensions. Further, because it is a religious monument things have to be done in the right way. It is a hollow structure, and the right objects have to be chosen to put inside, in the right order, blessed, prayers said over them and so on and so forth, so it is quite a complex cultural activity in every sense. In talking to people in Bhutan we found somebody who would be interested and we agreed that if we were going to do it at all, we were going to do it properly. Our Stupa is genuine, made exactly as it would have been in Bhutan or Nepal or Tibet or anywhere in that part of the world.

Actually, places like Harewood are full of things which are not English. People think of a completely English country garden but actually they are often full of plants which are not English at all. Rhododendrons for example, are not an English plant they are a Himalayan plant so I felt that the Stupa tied into that, to those historic connections if you like, how a landscape like Harewood evolved, which is actually much more internationally multicultural than might at first meet the eye.

I had no idea how it would actually work, it was a leap into the unknown, all of this. The guys who came over to build it had never left their own country, never been in an aeroplane, never left their own culture. Bhutan is a land-locked state, they had never seen the sea. One of the highlights of their visit was taking them all to eat fish and chips in Whitby and walk on the beach. So it was a leap in the dark from that point of view but I think it has worked amazingly well. The Stupa looks as if it has always been there. That bit of the garden which I have always loved, the sunken garden, used to be called the rock garden, now the Himalayan garden. Trevor Nicholson, the Head Gardener here, also has travelled quite a lot in the Himalayas and has been on plant hunting expeditions and so on and had been talking for a while about wanting to turn that into an exclusively Himalayan garden and that's the way the Stupa has kicked that on into the next phase.

What are some other events that were memorable, although not as memorable or historic?

In terms of historic significance I think that the separation of the Estate and the Trust is very important. I think the buildings at Harewood Yard were very significant in terms of converting those farm buildings into what they are now. Prior to the renovations, the buildings were falling down, mixed in with them were lots of very ugly asbestos roof farm buildings. It was no longer possible to use it for farming. If we had wanted to go on with Home Farm, we physically couldn't have got modern equipment in through the gates, you would have had to knock the whole frontage down, which was just impractical. So I think those conversions, which happened over several years, were very significant and to me very exciting as it has completely re-invigorated that whole part of the Estate.

The Turner exhibition was certainly a big one. I am a big supporter of the contemporary art programme here and although Turner is not a contemporary artist himself, he is an inspiration to many contemporary artists because in his time he was enormously innovative. It is important for Harewood to be about 'now' and not just about 'then' or 'yesterday'. It has to mean something to a range of people today and not just people who are interested in 18th Century building or design – that interest is almost a given, but to me that is the starting point, not the end point of what we do here.

Can I introduce another one for you? That, of course, is the stables.

I was going to say that the other big building projects included the re-roofing of the House which was a big project but not so glamorous. The stables was a huge building project.

Was it coincidence that it was exactly 250 years from the time when it was originally built?

Actually it was, completely coincidental. I don't think we realised it until after the event took place. Again a similar history in some ways, although it was not in quite as bad condition as the old Home Farm was, but it was in pretty bad condition and needed re-inventing. It still has a few minor problems that are inevitable in any public building, but I am very excited with the popular potential that it has built up. I am also very excited by the mixture of old and new, the fact that it has been immaculately restored on the outside but is very crisp and modern on the inside. The inside was in pretty poor condition, and most of the old features had disappeared or were completely irrelevant because it was never going to be a stables again, or even a garage which it was in the 30s onwards. So I am excited by that, again that sort of old and new thing, finding ways of making Harewood be at the forefront of design and usage and so on. We have been nominated for an award for it actually – Georgian award for best use of a Georgian building.

I would enjoy hearing your views about the Castle conservation project.

It was sort of 'invisible mending' which is very much the current archaeological approach to buildings like that, not to intervene. For example, a lot of big plants were left growing out of it because they had become part of the fabric of the building. The dilemma with the Castle has always been that it is in quite an inaccessible site, quite an awkward site to get around, even once you do actually get there, it's a very steep hill. It is not ever going to be a major visitor attraction and to make it accessible to all would be extremely expensive and just doesn't make any economic sense. The plan is to have accompanied visits there, and there have been one or two from special interest groups already. It is just not practical to have a car park in there, or even to make a wheelchair friendly footpath, the logistics are horrendous. It is a fascinating building, a lot of work has been done on it and a lot of historical and archaeo-logical discoveries were made in the process of restoration which will be made available. There will be off-site displays or maybe computer mock-ups of how it might have been, but it is never going to be a hugely visited, easily accessible visitor attraction.

What about All Saints Church, do you have any views?

Well, All Saints Church actually belongs to the Churches Conservation Trust and its use has been stepped up a little bit in recent years and that will continue to happen, but in the end it is their responsibility. It is still conse-crated so it is used for weddings, sometimes for blessings, memorial services or harvest festivals, carol services and so on. It is also a wonderful venue for performances, with lovely acoustics. It has been used for art on a few occasions. We are working with the Churches Conservation Trust to try to make it a bit more user friendly in the winter, i.e. put some heating into it because it is incredibly cold!

I'd like to see it used more, it is a lovely building and the Churches people are pretty flexible about what it is used for, it is a two way thing between Harewood and the Churches Conservation Trust. In other words, Harewood can certainly suggest a whole range of things that could go on there, but what we can't do is invest a lot of money in the fabric of the place and it is not our responsibility. But we have a good relationship with them which is ongoing so I think it will only get better

So, if I can summarise, the future is about living for today without forget-ting about tomorrow, it is being present for people today without turning it into a Disneyesque theme park and Harewood is not interested at all in things which have the potential to be 'boom and bust'. But, last year the Trust hosted pop concerts that caused more than a bit of a stir, and some problems, in Harewood village. What are your views?

In order to make ends meet we are going to continue to have to have a certain number of big events each year, it is an economic necessity. We have had concerts before, last year was by far the biggest we have ever had and lessons were learned to do with access and particularly exit, especially to do with timing, days of the week and so on. We are going to have to continue with those sorts of events and you have got to learn from the things that we got right, which was quite a lot of things, and also some things which were not quite right and there have been extensive de-briefings. There will probably be similar things next year. But these things go in cycles, they go in and out of fashion as it were, and we will go in or out of fashion as a venue, but they have been a pretty crucial financial underpinning frankly over the last couple of years.

Is there anything else you would like to tell me?

The final thing I would like to say, which is important, is a kind of further spin on what you were saying about access and so on, I think it is important that we become accessible to as wide a range of people as possible, given the kind of area we live in, and the enormous range of races and types of people who live in the area. For many people, coming to Harewood would not be a natural thing. 2007 is the bicentenary of the abolition of the slave trade so there are going to be a lot of things happening across the country for that, Bristol, Liverpool, Hull, the Wilberforce connection. We are being very active in doing things here and a lot of the programming and the temporary exhibitions will relate to that in some way or other. Not in terms of exhibitions about the history of the slave trade because other people will be doing that bigger and better than we possibly could, but we are very much acknowledging it and there will be a series of performances in September in a big tent – 20,000 people over three weeks. It will be called Carnival Messiah – Handel's Messiah done carnival style. I am very excited about it.

I am keen for Harewood to be seen as something that is as inclusive and welcoming to people as possible without changing its basic nature. That's the challenge and there are contradictions in that but it is an interesting challenge and we will take steps, one at a time, towards making that happen. So, that's my long term aim.

Given the consistency of David Lascelles's 'vision' for Harewood over such an extended period of time, and his obvious energy and enthusiasm for the job he has before him, I am sure that we will all look forward to seeing the next chapters in the 'Harewood story' as they unfold.

CHAPTER SEVEN
Harewood Comparative History
1066–2007

The Doric Arch at the entrance to Harewood House

Introduction

In this Chapter, I have compared various events in the 'life' of Harewood with what was happening elsewhere – key events in history, when famous people were born or died, when significant inventions took place, when well known organisations were created, famous songs first sung and so on. In general, a highly eclectic selection.

I have included three "other events" for each year in Harewood's history. Given that I have listed over one hundred separate years that had some significance to Harewood, the task of finding over three hundred comparative events was more than a bit challenging!

As I'm sure you will appreciate, it was not always possible to match an exact date in Harewood's history with events elsewhere and therefore a selection of events as close to the Harewood dates as possible are presented, with the relevant years shown (if no year is shown against the 'Events Elsewhere' it is the same as the 'Harewood Event' date in Column 1). In other years, it was very difficult to decide which three events to include because so much was happening in the world. I have therefore attempted to use a wide-ranging selection so that there will hopefully be something of interest to everyone.

I have used countless websites and books as source material for this Chapter. The research has been absolutely fascinating and I made many interesting discoveries!

I hope you will enjoy reading this Chapter as much as I enjoyed researching it!

What Happened When?

Year	Harewood Event	Events Elsewhere
1066	• Whilst the history of Harewood began at the time of the Bronze Age, I have called 1066 the 'official' start date as this is when the written history of Harewood, for the most part, began.	• Battle of Hastings. • Christmas Day – the coronation of King William I at Westminster Abbey. • Bayeaux Tapestry commissioned 1066-1077.
1086	• At the time of the Domesday Book Harewood belonged to Tor, Sprot and Grimm, three Saxon Chieftains. It was then given by William the Conqueror to Robert de Romelli as reward for his support in 1094.	• Domesday Book is completed in England. • The Imam Ali Mosque in Najaf, Iraq, is rebuilt by the Seljuk Malik Shah I after being destroyed by fire. • 1087 the first Crusade to reverse Islamic gains in the Middle East begins.
1116	• All Saints Church founded by William de Curci.	• 1100 establishment of the Latin kingdom of Jerusalem. • 1107 King Henry I and the Pope agree that the former should invest bishops with their temporal authority and the latter with spiritual authority. • 1118 birth of Thomas a Becket – Archbishop of Canterbury and saint. He was murdered in 1170.

1135	• The last representative of the Gawthorpe family, Maud, married William Gascoigne. By this marriage Gawthorpe became the property and residence of the Gascoignes.	• The death of Henry I and the coronation of his nephew Stephen. • 1141 King Stephen captured by the Scots at Lincoln but the fight was continued by his wife Matilda. • 1147 start of the second Crusade.
1209	• King John granted a Charter to Warin Fitz Gerald, his chamberland, who by his marriage to Alicia (or Alice) de Curci, became the Lord of the Manor.	• 1187 Saladin defeats Crusaders at the Battle of Hattin (between Damascus and Jerusalem). • 1204 King John surrenders Normandy to the French king. • 1215 signing of the Magna Carta at Runnymede.
1307	• All Saints Church badly damaged during Scottish raids.	• 1306 Robert Bruce is crowned as King of Scotland. • Legend states that this is the year when William Tell shot the apple off his son's head. • Edward II became King of England on the death of his father, Edward I.
1310	• Robert de Lisle was allotted the manor of Harewood from his cousin Isabel.	• 1308 Edward II married Isabella of France in January. The following month was his coronation. • First purpose-built accommodation for students completed at Merton College, Oxford. • 1312 Pope Clement V is said to have forcibly disbanded the Knights Templar on Friday 13th October which is rumoured to be the basis of the 'Friday 13th' stigma.
1315	• Reference is made to the first of the Harewood line of Lascelles in the document Loidis et Elmet.	• The Battle of Bannockburn took place on 24th June 1314. This was one of the most spectacular battles of the Scottish Wars of Independence from the English crown. The victory secured the future of the throne for Robert the Bruce, King of Scots. • 1315-17 Great Famine in Northern Europe. • 1318 Edward Bruce, younger brother of Robert the Bruce, was killed in battle.
1356	• Edward Balliol, very close friend of Sir William Aldburgh of Harewood Castle, was forced to surrender his claim to the Scottish throne to Edward III.	• 1354 Ottomans capture Gallipoli and gain first foothold in Europe. • 19th September 1356 the Battle of Poitiers took place. This was the second of the three great English victories of the Hundred Years' War (1337-1453). The other two were

		Crécy and Agincourt.
		• Edward III burned down every town and village in Lothian, Scotland.
1363	• Edward Balliol died, possibly in Yorkshire.	• 1359 Birth of Owen Glendower – last independent Prince of Wales and Welsh nationalist. He died in 1415. • 1361 Edirne (Adrianople) taken; becomes new Ottoman capital. • Second plague pandemic in Europe (1362-63).
1366	• Edward II granted a licence to William de Aldburgh to fortify his new castle on Harewood Bank. He had held the manor since 1364.	• Foundation of the Stella Artois brewery in present-day Belgium. • 1381 Wycliffe writes his heretical *Confessio.* • 1381 the Peasants' Revolt is suppressed.
1388	• Sir William Aldburgh died. As he had no children, the castle passed to his two sisters whose families jointly owned the castle for nearly three centuries.	• 1384 first complete handwritten manuscript of English bible finished by John Wycliffe. • 1389 Battle of Kosovo: Ottoman supremacy in the Balkans established. • 1399 the Lancastrian Henry IV succeeds the deposed King Richard II.
1407	• Sir Richard Redman obtained a grant for a fair and free warren – sole right to kill game on the estate.	• 1400 Chaucer dies leaving his Canterbury Tales unfinished. • *Statute de Heretico Comburendo* confirms the punishment of burning for heretics. • 1413 Henry IV died leaving relations with France and internal politics almost equally confused.
1419	• Lord Chief Justice, Sir William Gascoigne died.	• 1415, 25th October, Battle of Agincourt – King Henry V defeats the French. • Dick Whittington became Lord Mayor of London for the 3rd time. He died in 1423. • 1422 birth of William Caxton – prose writer, translator and printer. He died in 1491.
1424	• All Saints church was reopened after extensive alterations.	• 1422 King Henry V died. • 1429 Joan of Arc has an audience with Charles VII of France. She was burnt at the stake in Rouen in the Old Market Square in 1431. • 1429 Charles VII crowned in the Cathedral in Rhiems.
1445	• Sir William Ryther got a patent for a market, fair and free warren in Harewood.	• 1441 Eton College founded by Henry VI. • Birth of Cardinal Thomas Wolsey – Statesman to King Henry VIII. He died in 1530.

		• 1453 final English defeats bring the Hundred Years' War to a close.
1633	• Lord Strafford obtained a confirmation of all previous grants for warren in Harewood.	• William Laud becomes Archbishop of Canterbury. • Birth of Samuel Pepys – diarist and government official. He died in 1703. • 1634 saw the first of the 10 yearly Passion Plays being performed at Ober-Ammergau.
1648	• The beginning of the Lascelles involvement in the West Indies.	• The Preston Campaign of the English Civil Wars took place. • The celebrated wood-carver whose work adorns St Paul's Cathedral, Grinling Gibbons was born. He died in 1721. • The composer Michael East died. He was born in 1580.
1653	• The Lascelles family moved from Hinderskelfe to Northallerton. • Francis Lascelles was Colonel in the Parliamentary Army.	• 1652 Death of Inigo Jones – regarded as the first significant English architect. He was born in 1573. • Cromwell dismisses parliament and becomes protector. • Izaak Walton (1593-1683) – English writer, wrote his famous book *The Complete Angler* in 1653.
1656	• Harewood's market or town hall is rumoured to have been pulled down. • William Strafford, son of the ill-fated Earl of Strafford, was forced to sell Harewood Castle and Gawthorpe Hall because of debt.	• Cromwell allows the Jews to return to England. • Birth of Edmond Halley – English astronomer, geophysicist, mathematician, meteorologist and physicist. He died in 1742. • 1657 Foundation of the General Post Office.
1675	• Ivy Cottage, the oldest building in Harewood, still standing, was built.	• 1670 the Treaty of Dover creates an alliance between France and Britain against the Dutch. • 1673 Catholics and Nonconformists are forbidden to hold public office by the Test Act. • Foundation of Greenwich Observatory.
1678	• This year is inscribed on the lintel over the door in what is known as Cutler's Cottage.	• Titus Oates fabricates the 'Popish Plot'. This was an alleged Catholic conspiracy. In fact, the plot was devised to discredit Catholics in England. • 1679 The Habeas Corpus Amendment Act is passed, giving some protection against imprisonment without trial. • 1682 William Penn leaves England to found Pennsylvania in what was to become the United States.

1696	• The Harewood and Gawthorpe estates passed into the hands of John Boulter, a kinsman of John Cutler.	• 1694 Foundation of the Bank of England. • 1695 Death of Henry Purcell – music composer. He was born in 1659. • 1697 Birth of William Hogarth – painter and printmaker. He died in 1764.
1703	• Harewood's Market Cross was re-erected by John Boulter.	• 1701 The Act of Settlement is passed, thus securing an eventual Protestant Hanoverian succession. • Death of Robert Hooke – experimental philosopher, scientist and architect. He was born in 1635. • Birth of John Wesley – religious reformer. He died in 1791.
1729	• The current Harewood Bridge was built.	• 1728 Birth of Robert Adam – architect and interior designer. He died in 1792. • 1728 Birth of Captain Cook – seaman, explorer and cartographer. He died in 1779. • 1732 10 Downing Street becomes the residence of the First Lord of the Treasury and Prime Minister.
1739	• John Boulter's son Edmund was forced by debt to sell the estates of Harewood and Gawthorpe to Henry Lascelles.	• 1737 Birth of Tom Paine – political philosopher. He died in 1809. • 1737 Birth of Edward Gibbon – historian. He died in 1794. • Dick Turpin hanged for murder.
1740	• The house of William Wright of Harewood was registered in the Registry of the Archbishop of York as a place of religious worship for the Quakers.	• War of Austrian Succession begins against France and Spain. • 1741 Foundation of the Founding Hospital by Captain Thomas Coram. • 1745 God Save the King first performed by way of support for George II after the defeat of his army by the Jacobites.
1743	• The commission house of Lascelles and Maxwell was established in London.	• Henry Pelham (1694-1754), Whig Statesman, became Prime Minister. • The premiere in London of George Frederic Handel's oratorio, *Samson*. • King George II leads the British army to victory at Dettingen. This was known as the War of Austrian Succession or King George's War against the French.
1748	• Edwin Lascelles was installed as Lord of the Manor of Harewood by his father, Henry, who owned the estate.	• Adam Smith, Scottish Economist (depicted on the back of the Bank of England £20 in 2007), begins to deliver public lectures in Edinburgh. • William Kent, an eminent English architect, landscape architect and furniture designer of the early 18th century died. He was born in Yorkshire in 1685.

		Yorkshire in 1685. • Isaac Watts, 'father' of English hymn-writing died. He was born in 1674.
1753	• Edwin Lascelles inherited the estates of Gawthorpe and Harewood upon the death of his father, Henry. • The toll bar riots arose out of the discontent and opposition of the Turnpike Act.	• The British Museum was established. It opened to the public in 1759. • The first official St Patrick's Day celebrations took place at the Crown and Thistle Tavern in New York City. • 1754 foundation of the Royal and Ancient Golf Club.
1755	• Edwin Lascelles created a short lived ribbon factory in an attempt to add more employment to the village. • Work commenced on building the stables for Gawthorpe Hall.	• Birth of Josiah Spode – ceramics retailer and master potter. He died in 1827. • 1756 Seven Years War begins against France. • 1758 birth of Lord Nelson – naval commander and national hero. He died in 1805.
1759	• The building of New Gawthorpe Hall (Harewood House) began. • Foundation stone laid by Edwin Lascelles.	• Birth of William Pitt the Younger – Prime Minister. He died in 1806. • Birth of Robert Burns – poet. He died in 1796. • Joseph Haydn (1732-1809), one of the most prominent composers of the classical period, composed his Symphony no 1 in D Major.
1760	• This year marked the peak of the number of public houses in Harewood – six.	• Birth of William Wilberforce – abolitionist of slavery. He died in 1833. • George II, the last British monarch to have been born outside Great Britain died. He was born in 1683. • 1763 Peace of Paris confirms most of Britain's overseas gains, notably in Canada and India.
1767	• Reverend Ismay visited Harewood.	• John Newbery, an English publisher who specialised in children's books died. He was baptized in 1713 but his exact birth date not known. • 1766 birth of Thomas Malthus – economist and demographer. He died in 1834. • 1766 birth of John Dalton – chemist and formulator of atomic theory to explain chemical reactions. He died in 1844.
1768	• Edwin Lascelles built a school with two houses for teachers.	• Foundation of the Royal Academy of Arts. • 1769 birth of the Duke of Wellington – military commander and statesman. He died in 1852. • 1770 birth of William Wordsworth –

		poet. He died in 1850.
1771	• Harewood House was completed.	• 1770 Captain Cook lands in Australia. • Birth of Walter Scott – novelist and poet. He died in 1832. • Thomas Grey, English poet, classical scholar and professor of Cambridge University died. He was born in 1716.
1772	• Methodism came to Harewood, with services being held in private houses until a chapel was built in 1815. • Capability Brown began working on the Harewood Estate.	• Birth of Samuel Taylor Coleridge – poet, philosopher and critic. He died in 1834. • Death of John Canton (1718–1772). English physicist who was the first in England to verify Benjamin Franklin's hypothesis of the identity of lightening and electricity. • 1773 The Boston Tea Party. This was an act of protest by the American colonies against Britain for unfair tax and lack of representation in Westminster Parliament.
1774	• Historians believe that Thomas Chippendale only visited Harewood House twice, September 1774 and February 1776.	• Death of Oliver Goldsmith – Irish writer and physician. He was born in 1730. • Birth of Robert Southey – English poet of the Romantic school, one of the 'Lake Poets' and Poet Laureate. He died in 1843. • Continental Congress – federal legislature of the Thirteen Colonies – drafts 'Declaration of Rights and Grievances'.
1783	• Capability Brown died. This was only one year after his last bill for work carried out on the Harewood Estate was finally paid!	• Tyburn Hill last used as a place of execution in London. • Beethoven's first printed works are published. • Revolutionary War between the United Kingdom and the United States comes to an end with Treaty of Paris.
1784	• Daniel Lascelles dies heirless.	• First mail coach runs from Bristol to London. • Death of Samuel Johnson – one of England's greatest literary figures: a poet, essayist, biographer and lexicographer. He was born in 1709. • John Wesley created his 'Deed of Declaration', the basic work of Methodism.
1786	• Younger brother of Daniel, Henry dies childless.	• 1785 Russians settle Aleutian Islands. • 1787 the Constitution of the US signed.

		• 1787 Mozart's *Don Giovanni* premiered in Prague.
1790	• Edwin Lascelles was ennobled with the title of Baron Harewood of Harewood Castle.	• President George Washington gives the first State of the Union Address. • HMS *Bounty* mutineers settle on Pitcairn Island. • 1791 foundation of the Ordnance Survey.
1793	• Restoration work took place at All Saints Church.	• Revolutionary France declares war on Britain. • John de Groat and his 2 brothers settled in what is now known as 'John o'Groats'. • The Louvre opens in Paris.
1795	• Edwin Lascelles died, and the family vault was created under All Saints Church. • The Harewood Estate passed to Edwin's cousin, Edward Lascelles.	• Birth of Charles Barry – architect. He died in 1860. • Birth of Thomas Carlyle – historian and essayist. He died in 1881. • 1796 Edward Jenner introduces smallpox vaccination.
1797	• Edward Lascelles took his seat in the House of Lords.	• Mutiny in the Navy at Spithead over poor living conditions on Royal Navy vessels and inadequate pay. • Birth of Mary Shelley – English romantic/gothic novelist, the author of 'Frankenstein'. Married to romantic poet Percy Bysshe Shelley. She died in 1851. • Napoleon conquers Austrian Lombardy and Venice.
1798	• J M W Turner painted Harewood Castle from both Southerly and Northerly perspectives.	• 1797 the Royal College of Surgeons is incorporated by Royal Charter. • Battle of the Nile took place in Aboukir Bay, Egypt. This was an important naval battle of the French Revolutionary wars between the British fleet commanded by Rear-Admiral Horatio Nelson and the French under Vice-Admiral Francois-Paul Brueys D'Aigalliers. • Napoleon extends French conquests to Rome and Egypt.
1799	• The road that climbed Harewood Bank, around the perimeter of Harewood Castle, was built. Now the A61.	• 1798 the Irish rebellion is quelled. • Income Tax introduced in the United Kingdom. • Rosetta Stone discovered in Egypt.
1801	• The Doric entrance to the park (Harewood Estate) was designed by Carr and executed in this year by John Muschamp, the village mason.	• Union of Great Britain and Ireland took effect – Act passed in 1800. • First National Census in the UK. • Birth of Cardinal Newman – theologian, cleric and educationalist. He died in 1890.
1804	• The Market Cross in Harewood was taken down and destroyed.	• Napoleon transforms the Consulate of France into an empire,

		proclaiming himself Emperor of France.
		• Lewis and Clark expedition begins exploration of what is now North West US.
		• 1805 Lord Nelson defeats the French-Spanish fleets in the Battle of Trafalgar.
1807	• Wordsworth wrote his poem, *The Founding of Bolton Priory*, referring to the death of young Romelli. Published in 1808.	• British Parliament passes the Act which marked the beginning of the end of Britain's participation in the slave trade.
		• First national census of the population is taken.
		• London's Pall Mall is the first street to be lit by gaslight.
1810	• The Harewood Arms – inn and public house – was built.	• 1809 birth of Charles Darwin – natural historian and evolutionist. He died in 1882.
		• 1809 Birth of Alfred Lord Tennyson – poet. He died in 1892.
		• 1809 Birth of William Ewart Gladstone – politician and Prime Minister. He died in 1898.
1812	• Edward created first Earl of Harewood, establishing the dynasty that continues to flourish seven generations on.	• Napoleon's Grand Army invades Russia in June.
		• In the US war with Britain declared over freedom of the seas for US vessels – War of 1812.
		• Birth of Charles Dickens. He died in 1870.
1815	• Two dwelling houses were converted into a Methodist Chapel in Harewood.	• Napoleon defeated by Wellington at Waterloo and took exile in St Helena.
		• War of 1812 ends with Treaty of Ghent.
		• Sir Humphrey Davey of London patented the miner's safety lamp.
1816	• The Tsar of Russia visited Harewood.	• Charlotte Bronte was born. She died in 1855.
		• 1817 Jane Austen died. She was born in 1775.
		• 1818 Karl Marx was born. He died in 1883.
1820	• Edward, the 1st Earl, died.	• 1819 Singapore founded by Britain as free trade port.
		• 1819 The 'Peterloo Massacre' in Manchester takes place when troops fire on a demonstration.
		• Florence Nightingale was born. She died in 1910.
1835	• Duchess of Kent and Princess Victoria visited Harewood.	• 1834 The Tolpuddle Martyrs are transported to Australia.
		• 1834 The Poor Law Amendment Act

		is passed. • Mark Twain was born. He died in 1910.
1840	• The first year in which Lord Harewood and his extended household are said to have travelled by train for their annual pilgrimage to and from London.	• Penny postage is introduced. • Claude Monet – famous French impressionist painter was born. He died in 1926. • Queen Victoria marries Prince Albert.
1841	• The 2nd Earl died.	• Hong Kong proclaimed as sovereign territory of Britain. • Thomas Cook opens first travel agency. • 'Punch' magazine first published.
1842	• The finished drawings for the renovation of Harewood House were submitted by Sir Charles Barry. Barry's work completely altered the character of the house.	• Birth of Sir Arthur Sullivan – English composer best known for his operatic collaborations with librettist W S Gilbert. He died in 1900. • Death of Grace Darling – one of England's best-loved Victorian heroines. She and her father rescued 9 survivors from the ship 'Forfarshire' in 1838 in weather too rough for lifeboats. She was born in 1815. • Crawford Long uses first anesthetic – ether.
1845	• The school built by Edwin Lascelles was replaced by one provided by the 3rd Earl of Harewood, and his Countess supplied all the books and equipment.	• 1847 birth of Alexander Graham Bell – telephone and aeronautics engineer and inventor of aids for teaching the deaf. He died in 1922. • 1848 birth of W G Grace – cricketer and doctor. He died in 1915. • 1848 death of Emily Bronte – novelist and poet. She was born in 1818.
1853	• A Literary and Scientific Institution was formed in a partially occupied house next to the Village Shop and Post Office. (This building is now the village chapel.)	• 1851 death of J M W Turner – artist. He was born in 1775. • 1851 The Great Exhibition in London. • 1854 birth of Oscar Wilde – dramatist and poet. He died in 1900.
1857	• The 3rd Earl died.	• Robert Baden-Powell was born. He died in 1941. • Edward Elgar was born. He died in 1934. • World's first soccer club, Sheffield FC, founded.
1862	• Major restoration work began at All Saints Church.	• Henry David Thoreau died. He was born in 1817. • Westminster Bridge across River Thames opens. • Lewis Carroll creates Alice in Wonderland.

1892	• The 4th Earl died.	• Ellis Island begins accepting immigrants to the United States. • William Ewart Gladstone assumes British premiership as head of a Liberal government with Irish Nationalist Party support. • Diesel engine invented by Rudolf Diesel and patented by him in this year.
1901	• Electricity was installed in Harewood House.	• King Edward VII ascends the British throne on the death of his mother Queen Victoria. • A showing of 71 Vincent van Gogh paintings in Paris, 11 years after his death, creates a sensation. • The Royal Navy's first submarine was launched at Barrow.
1908	• King Edward VIII visited Harewood.	• Paper cups launched by the International Paper Co, New York. • Ford's Model T rolls off the assembly line. • Gideon Bible Company started.
1915	• Harewood House is turned into an auxiliary hospital for officers by Lord Harewood who was the President of the West Riding Territorial Association.	• Second Battle of Ypres took place in which the Germans used poison gas for the first time. • The British oceanliner Lusitania sunk by a German submarine. • Harry Ramsden opens his first fish and chip shop in Bradford.
1916	• This year changed the life of Lord Lascelles (who would become the 6th Earl) significantly. Shortly after a brief meeting with his great uncle, the 2nd Marquess of Clanricarde in London the Marquess died and left his very significant estate to Lord Lascelles.	• William Boeing founded his aircraft construction company. • Albert Einstein publishes his 'theory of relativity'. • German and British navies clash in the Battle of Jutland, the largest naval battle of WWI.
1919	• The Harewood Women's Institute (WI), one of the first in the country, was established. It was finally disbanded in 2005.	• Sir Edwin Lutyens' war memorial, the Cenotaph, is unveiled in Whitehall. • First post-war performance at Covent Garden: Beecham conducts Puccini's 'La Boheme'. • Nancy Astor became Britain's first woman MP.
1921	• The 6th Lord Harewood became engaged to the Princess Mary in November of this year.	• Queen Mary is the first woman to be awarded a degree from Oxford University when she receives an honorary degree. • In March a state of emergency is declared in the UK after a coal strike is called. • On 9th September Charlie Chaplin returned for a visit to the city of his

		• birth, London.
1922	• Henry Lascelles, 6th Earl, married Princess Mary, daughter of King George V.	• British Egyptologist Howard Carter discovers the tomb of Tutankamun. • The Fascists march on Rome and Mussolini becomes leader of Italy. • The BBC begins radio service in the UK.
1923	• The 7th Earl, George, was born.	• In New York the first public showing takes place of a 'sound on film' picture. • The Duke of York and Lady Elizabeth Bowes-Lyon are married. • 8th May Jack Hobbs completed his 100th century in first-class cricket.
1928	• H H Griffith became the vicar of All Saints Church.	• Death of Thomas Hardy – novelist and poet. He was born in 1840. • The final draft of the revised Book of Common Prayer is issued. • Women over 21 were given the right to vote in the UK.
1929	• The 5th Earl died.	• The New York Stock Exchange crashed and triggered the Great Depression. • First Academy Awards presented. • Guy Lombardo plays 'Auld Lang Syne' for the first time.
1930	• The 6th Earl moved to Harewood from Goldsborough Hall.	• First football World Cup, won by host Uruguay. • British aviator Amy Johnson was the first woman to make a solo flight from London to Australia. • The House of Commons votes to raise the school leaving age to 15.
1932	• The 6th Earl's wife, HRH Princess Mary, became The Princess Royal.	• Actress Elizabeth Taylor was born. • The BBC makes its first broadcast from the new Broadcasting House. • King George V makes the first royal Christmas Day broadcast to the Empire.
1935	• On 6th May Silver Jubilee Celebrations for the King and Queen (King George V and Queen Mary) took place at Harewood Park.	• 'Cat's Eyes', invented by Percy Shaw, are first used on British roads. • 19th May Colonel T E Lawrence (Lawrence of Arabia) died following a motorcycle accident. • Sir Malcolm Campbell set a new world record of over 300 miles per hour in his car Bluebird.
1937	• The Earl of Harewood granted permission for a Masonic Lodge to use the name Harewood, subject to it being pronounced as 'Harwood'.	• Margot Fonteyn debuts in 'Giselle' at Sadler's Wells. • Famous people born this year include: Anthony Hopkins, Bill Cosby, Colin Powell, Dustin Hoffman, Jack Nicholson, Jane Fonda, Robert Redford, Shirley

		Bassey, Morgan Freeman and Warren Beatty.
		• King George VI and Queen Elizabeth were crowned at Westminster Abbey.
1939	• Harewood House became a convalescent hospital once again. • Harewood News reports that 'Harewood Village Hall Plans Go Through'.	• The year World War II began. • Frank J Whittle invents the jet engine. • Robert Watson-Watt invents radar.
1942	• The Earl of Harewood became Grand Master of the Harewood Masonic Lodge.	• Earl Tupper uses polyethylene to create Tupperware. • A sell-by-date is first used on Lyons coffee in Britain. • Italian physicist Enrico Fermi launches the first controlled nuclear chain reaction at the University of Chicago.
1947	• The 6th Earl died.	• The Edinburgh Festival is launched. • Mikhail Kalashnikov invents the AK-47. • The Dead Sea Scrolls are discovered by a Bedouin shepherd in Jordan.
1949	• Princess Elizabeth and the Duke of Edinburgh visited Harewood. • The Earl of Harewood married his first wife, Marion Stein.	• The entire Tate Gallery is opened again for the first time since 1939. • Olivier's 'Hamlet' became the first British film to win an Academy Award for Best Picture. • Chocolate and sweet rationing ends in the UK.
1950	• Harewood House became open to the public.	• Frank Sinatra made his London debut at the London Palladium. • British troops join US forces in Korea. • Mother Theresa founded her Mission of Charity in Calcutta, India.
1953	• Christening of the Earl's second son took place at All Saints Church, Harewood.	• 25th March Queen Mary dies in her sleep. • 2nd June Queen Elizabeth II is crowned. • Queen Elizabeth II launches the new Royal Yacht, Britannia.
1959	• Harewood's Village Hall was officially opened by HRH The Princess Royal and the Countess of Harewood. • On 2nd to 5th September, the Harewood Horse Trials European Championships took place at Harewood.	• Fidel Castro takes power in Cuba. • Alec Issigonis's Morris Mini is launched. • Briton Christopher Cockerell launches the hovercraft.
1961	• The two hundred year old bar house built by John Carr, on the north side of the river bridge, was pulled down.	• Yuri Gagarin became the first man in space. • A coup, backed by the CIA and

		President John F Kennedy, fails at the Bay of Pigs in Cuba. • The Berlin Wall was built.
1962	• The year of the great gale in which a tremendous number of trees in Harewood, including some fine elms, were destroyed. • On 17th March the Combined Charities Fashion Show took place at Harewood House.	• Cuban Missile Crisis. • John Glenn becomes the first American to orbit earth in space. • The Beatles debut with 'Love Me Do'.
1964	• The dedication service for the new Methodist Chapel took place in April.	• Cassius Clay (Mohammed Ali) became the World Heavyweight Boxing Champion. • Nelson Mandela sentenced to life imprisonment for treason. • Vatican abolishes Latin as official language of Roman Catholic liturgy.
1965	• The Princess Royal died.	• US troops deployed in Vietnam – anti-war protests start. • Ray Dolby invents the Dolby sound recording system. • Sir Winston Churchill dies.
1967	• In July of this year Lord Harewood married Patricia Tuckwell (the Countess) in the United States.	• Donald Campbell dies on Coniston Water attempting to break the world water speed record. • The Queen opens the Queen Elizabeth Hall and the Purcell Room. • Barclay's Bank introduces Britain's first cash-dispensing machine.
1970	• The Sports and Social Club was built at the back of the Village Hall. • The bird garden and adventure playground opened at Harewood House.	• The Beatles split up. • IBM launches the floppy disc. • New English Bible launched, sells one million copies in first week.
1972	• The Harewood sawmill, owned by the Estate, was sold.	• Texas Instruments launches the pocket calculator. • Nike running shoes launched. • 'Bloody Sunday' takes place in Londonderry's Bogside.
1974	• The vicar of Harewood, the Reverend Canon H H Griffith died. • Harewood became part of Leeds Metropolitan District Council.	• Art Fry invents Post-It. • 13th June Prince Charles makes his maiden speech in the House of Lords, the first Royal Speech for 90 years. • Richard Nixon becomes the first US President to resign.
1975	• Last plantation in the Caribbean sold by the Lascelles.	• Margaret Thatcher becomes leader of the Conservative Party. • Vietnam War ends. • Queen Elizabeth II opens North Sea pipeline.
1976	• Lord Harewood sold three acres of land adjoining the park and the	• Viking I lands on Mars. • Konica introduces automatic focus

	Estate office. The development on this site became Harewood Mews.	camera. • Apple Computers founded by Steve Jobs and Stephen Wozniak.
1977	• All Saints Church officially declared redundant and services move to the Methodist Chapel on The Avenue.	• Space Shuttle makes its maiden flight. • Maria Callas died. She was born in 1923. • Queen Elizabeth II celebrates her Silver Jubilee.
1978	• All Saints Church became part of the Redundant Churches Fund (now the Churches Conservation Trust)Church • The book – *50 Years Gardening at Harewood* by Geoffrey Hall was published.	• Karol Wojtyla of Poland becomes Pope John Paul II. • Louise Brown became the first test-tube baby. • Superman the movie debuts, starring Christopher Reeve.
1981	• Lord Harewood's book – *The Tongs and the Bones*, was published. • Fragment of Anglo-Scandinavian cross shaft found during conservation of monuments at All Saints Church. • All Saints re-opened to the public.	• Prince Charles and Lady Diana Spencer marry. • The 'gang of four' launch the Social Democratic Party. • On 13th May Pope John Paul II is shot by a Turkish gunman.
1986	• The Country Landowners Association Game Fair came to Harewood for the first time. • Harewood became an educational charitable Trust.	• 28th January the space shuttle Challenger exploded after lift-off killing its crew of seven. • 'Tough guy' James Cagney dies on 30th March. • Richard Branson crosses the Atlantic in record time in the Virgin Atlantic Challenger II.
1989	• The former Sub Hall of Harewood House was refurbished specifically for use as an Art Gallery.	• George Bush Snr inaugurated as 41st US President. • Thousands killed in Tiananmen Square as Chinese leaders take hard line with demonstrators. • Dalai Lama wins Nobel Peace Prize.
1990	• *Select: Yorkshire Ridings Edition*, featured the restoration work being undertaken at Harewood House.	• South Africa frees Nelson Mandela. • Margaret Thatcher resigns as Prime Minister. • Iraqi troops invade Kuwait, setting off the Persian Gulf War.
1994	• Harewood's terrace gardens were developed and re-opened.	• Nelson Mandela elected President of South Africa. • The Church of England ordained its first female priests. • Change in Sunday trading laws – thousands of shops open.
1995	• Harewood developed its new watercolour rooms to showcase its own collections and to exhibit historic watercolours in the context for which they were originally intended.	• US shuttle docks with the Russian space station Mir. • Steve Fossett made the first solo transpacific balloon flight. • Drs Ian Wilmut and Keith Campbell create the world's first cloned sheep.
1997	• Emmerdale Village was built on the	• Hong Kong returns to Chinese rule

	Harewood Estate. • The first major exhibition in the watercolour rooms was 'Turner in the North' a collaboration with the Tate Gallery to celebrate the bicentenary of Turner's tour of the North of England which of course included Harewood House.	on 30th June. • Comet Hale-Bopp is the closest it will be to Earth until 4397. • Princess Diana killed in a car crash in Paris.
1998	• In April more than 200 staff members joined Lord and Lady Harewood in a photograph which brought back memories from Harewood House's past. Identical pictures were taken in 1930 and 1950 and the only person to have appeared in all three was Lord Harewood.	• Europeans agree on single currency, the *euro*. • Legendary crooner Frank Sinatra dies of a heart attack at age 82. • The US House of Representatives impeaches President Clinton on two charges, perjury and obstruction of justice.
2000	• The Chippendale exhibition was held at Harewood House. • £1m rescue plan for the Castle established.	• Concorde crash kills 113 near Paris. • Global warming talks collapse at Hague conference. • Nationwide uprising overthrows Yugoslavian President Milosevic.
2002	• The Queen visited Harewood Estate as part of her Golden Jubilee tour. • A major George Stubbs' drawings exhibition was held at Harewood House in the Terrace Gallery.	• Terrorist bomb in Bali kills hundreds. • Princess Margaret, free-spirited younger sister of the Queen, dies. • Former Yugoslav leader Slobodan Milosevic's trial begins in The Hague.
2003	• Sheep were replaced by red and roe deer in the park at the bottom of Church Lane. • Harewood successfully completed a Heritage Lottery Funded programme for secondary schools.	• Space shuttle *Columbia* explodes, killing all 7 astronauts. • The US and Britain launch war on Iraq. • European Union expands by 10 members.
2004	• Conservation work began on Harewood Castle. • The areas below stairs used by servants and staff of the House were opened as a new exhibition. A special area was devoted to the Princess Mary. • In conjunction with the Yorkshire Country House Partnership, the entire State Floor and Below Stairs became the platform for the 'Maids and Mistresses' exhibition. • Broadband came to Harewood.	• Spain's most horrific terrorist attack occurred killing 202. • New government formed in Iraq. • World leaders commemorate the 60th anniversary of D-Day.
2005	• Harewood Castle taken off the Buildings at Risk Register following completion of the conservation project. • HRH The Prince of Wales attended the consecration ceremony of the Harewood Stupa in the Himalayan	• Pope John Paul II dies in Rome. • London became the victim of terrorist bombings killing 52. • Hurricane Katrina slammed into the US Gulf Coast destroying towns in Mississippi and Louisiana.

	Garden.	
	• Harewood awarded title of 'most popular visitor attraction in Yorkshire'.	
	• Harewood WI disbanded.	
2006	• 'The Modern Show', staged in the Watercolour Rooms, brought 50 works of British Modern Art from private collections together, including pieces belonging to the Earl and Countess of Harewood and eight other collectors. • The O2 Wireless Festival came to Harewood.	• Hamas wins the majority of seats in the Palestinian Legislative Council elections. • The 1 billionth song is purchased from Apple iTunes Store. • Bristol celebrates the 200th birthday of Isambard Kingdom Brunel by relighting the Clifton Suspension Bridge.
2007	• Various events taking place at Harewood House, including Carnival Messiah in September, to mark the 200th anniversary of the end of slavery. • Yorkshire's first planetarium opened at Harewood House. • The Ice House (built in 1761) opened to the public for the first time following restoration. • CLA Game Fair cancelled for the first time in its 49 year history.	• Former communist countries admitted to European Union bringing the total to 27 countries. • Former Russian President Boris Yeltsin dies. • Large areas of England devastated by severe flooding following wettest Summer on record.

CHAPTER EIGHT
Olive Wild's Scrapbook
HRH Princess Mary 1930-1934

Jim Maxon, Author, with Olive Wild

Introduction

I interviewed Olive Wild on 7th March 2006. During our time together Olive told many, many stories about Harewood, but mostly about HRH Princess Mary and a variety of tales about Harewood House. Near the end of our chat Olive brought out her scrapbook that she had lovingly kept for the best part of five years about HRH Princess Mary and Harewood. Olive lent me the scrapbook and said that I could make a copy of it or do anything with it that I saw fit in relation to my book. Olive sadly died in December 2006 and therefore, nothing seemed more fitting than to include an edited version of her scrapbook within my book. I am grateful to her nephew, Anthony, for also giving his permission for this following Olive's death.

My wife and I became very close to Olive – in fact, she was one of the witnesses at our wedding in June 2006. I spoke to her countless times about how the book was coming along, but not once did I think to ask her why she began keeping her scrapbook in the first place and in particular why she suddenly stopped it. We shall never know because nothing in her scrapbook gave me any clues either.

Olive was born in 1911 and was brought up near Stratford upon Avon until her father got a job with the Harewood Estate in 1926. Although a 'southerner', she clearly threw herself into the village life of rural Yorkshire by joining all sorts of clubs and organisations and generally becoming part of the community as quickly as possible. She was 19 years old when she began her scrapbook.

Although I call it a scrapbook, which is precisely what it is, the title Olive wrote on the front cover of the 'book' was *Pictures of HRH Princess Mary then The Princess Royal*. However, the title inside the cover of the 'book' was *Pictures and Writing of Her Royal Highness Princess Mary, Countess of Harewood*. As far as the pictures go, most of them have been so badly worn over the years that it was not possible to scan any of them into my book.

I hope that you will not mind (and that the researchers amongst you will forgive me for this) but I have not been able to give exact references for the newspaper extracts I have included from Olive's scrapbook. The reason is that very few cuttings had so much as a date, let alone the name of the publication. It was only through reading each cutting together with what Olive had written that it was possible to deduce the approximate date of each cutting.

I am very grateful that Olive gave me permission to use her scrapbook and I am sure that you will find Olive's 'story' about HRH Princess Mary, as fascinating, insightful and humorous as I did. As you will see, Olive's words are in normal script and the extracts from newspaper cuttings are indented and appear in italics.

1930

Through the death of Lord Harewood in 1929, Her Royal Highness Princess Mary became our new Countess, now making the village of Harewood very popular.

> *Princess Mary's New Home – Villagers' Welcome Plans*
> *When Princess Mary and the Earl of Harewood come to Harewood, Yorkshire, on Saturday week to take up residence in Harewood House, it is probable that*

they will be accorded a reception from nearly all the villagers.

Although arrangements are not yet made, it is expected that they will be greeted at the gates of the park by tenants, and that their car will be pulled down the half-mile drive through the avenue of bronze beech trees to the wide doors of the hall.

This was the reception accorded to Princess Mary when she visited the hall after her engagement was announced.

New Royal Home and Yorkshire Welcome for Princess Mary
Mr Hibbert is polishing the big silver buttons of his green uniform. Mr Hibbert is one of the oldest servants on the Harewood Estate and lives in the lodge at the end of the half-mile sweep of tree-lined drive leading to the House.

He and the rest of the village of Harewood are preparing to welcome Princess Mary and the Earl of Harewood when they take up residence at Harewood next weekend.

Mr Hibbert's buttons are some of the largest one could find on a uniform. They are about the size of half a crown. Mr Hibbert is proud of them. They shine and glitter on his green uniform and each reflects a small picture of the sweep of drive and the trees as Mr Hibbert stands in front of his lodge door. Each one is so brightly polished that you would not believe they could be shinier.

"We are all glad that our Earl and the Princess are coming to Harewood" Mr Hibbert told me, and turned the full array of his silver buttons flashing upon me. "I opened the gates for King Edward when he was here, and I shall wear this uniform when the Earl and Countess arrive. I like it", he said.

The work of modernising the house will not be entirely finished when Princess Mary and the Earl of Harewood come to Harewood but it is expected that this will be completed shortly. The pony pets of Princess Mary's two sons, which they have ridden almost daily in the village streets of Goldsborough, will be brought to Harewood in a few days.

All the village is looking forward to the homecoming of the Earl and Countess. And Mr Hibbert is polishing his buttons.

Her Royal Highness Princess Mary and Lord Harewood arrived at Harewood on Saturday 25th October, to take up residence. Unluckily they had a smash on the way from Leeds but pleased no one was hurt.

Princess Mary in car smash with husband at crossroads – her coolness
(Leeds Sunday)
Princess Mary and the Earl of Harewood were involved in an alarming motor
accident when on their way from Leeds to Harewood House yesterday after-
noon. At the crossroads near Moortown, on the outskirts of the city, the car in
which the Princess and her husband were travelling came in collision with a
two-seater car driven by a woman. The impact was severe and both cars were
badly damaged. Happily neither car overturned and no-one was injured. I am
told that only the skill of the driver of Princess Mary's car averted a worse
smash. He managed to make the front of the car take the brunt of the impact.
The Princess displayed the coolness and courage of one who is accustomed to
take the stiff fences in the hunting field. She and her husband got out of the car
unassisted, and they stood chatting in the road until another car was sent to
take them to Harewood.

The Princess and Lord Harewood were travelling from London and they spent
the weekend at Harewood House where they are now in residence. The alter-
ations to Harewood House, which have been proceeding since the death of the
late Earl, are not yet completed, and the principal apartments are still in the
hands of the workmen. Until the alterations are completed, the Princess and
the Earl are temporarily occupying rooms in the west wing of the House.

Her Royal Highness and Lord Harewood are very popular in the hunting
field and both are liked by all. They attend church when they are at
Harewood House – Lord Harewood reads the lessons.

Her Royal Highness is very kind in all ways, especially giving prizes for all
good needs at dances etc.

Her Royal Highness and Lord Harewood attended church twice on
Christmas morning with quite a number of the house party. Princess Mary
looked charming.

Princess Mary's Guests – Quiet Festival at Harewood – Gifts from the
King and Queen
The Christmas of Princess Mary and Lord Harewood, the first they have spent
in residence at Harewood House, will be a quiet, old-fashioned country
festivity. The House and the village on the edge of the park are typical of the
surroundings in which Christmas can be celebrated in this way. The House
looks over wooded parkland to the grey Church which stands in the grounds,
and which Princess Mary and Lord Harewood will attend for morning service
on Christmas Day.

Princess Mary's two sons, the young Lord Lascelles and his brother Gerald, will have a particularly happy Christmas, for on Saturday their friends have been invited to a party. Lord and Lady Lloyd will be among the guests, and it is probable that both Lord Harewood and Princess Mary will attend the Boxing Day meeting of the Bramham Moor Hunt at Tadcaster.

Princess Mary's Sons at Hunt
Viscount Lascelles secured his first trophy when he attended the meet of the Bramham Moor Hunt with his parents on Christmas Eve. The Viscount was in at the kill and he was presented with the brush.

The Princess and the Earl, with their sons are in residence at Harewood House for their first Christmas, and yesterday morning the Princess and the Earl and the Viscount attended service in Harewood Church, and the Earl read the lessons. Peggy, Princess Mary's favourite Cairn terrier, was at the door of the church to greet her mistress when the service ended.

1931
Her Royal Highness celebrated her 34th birthday on 25th April 1931 while on her stay in London.

Princess Mary and Lord Harewood entertained a large house party for York Races, May 1931. All looked very nice when passing to go to the races.

Prince George came to Harewood House the last week in May and visited Leeds, etc.

Princess Mary has thrown the House and gardens open for charity – we have been down to see it, everything looks grand.

Lord Harewood attended a British Legion rally in Harewood Park on Saturday 4th July 1931. Lady Haig was also there.

HRH Princess Mary and her two sons were at church on Sunday 1st August – all look very nice.

Princess Mary has been very busy this week (August week) visiting Bridlington, Scarborough, Catterick Camp and Harrogate.

On Sunday 9th August, Her Royal Highness and a large number of visitors attended church. Lord Harewood read the lessons. The Princess looked beautiful.

On Monday 10th August, Princess Mary opened the Women's Institute Flower Show and presented the prizes afterwards. The Princess bought things from the stalls and was also a keen bidder when the auction sale was on. I am sure a very enjoyable evening was spent by everyone. The Princess caused much fun, she was so free with us all and was simply beautiful.

HRH and Lord Harewood entertained a large house party for York Races the last week in August 1931. Lord Lonsdale was one of the visitors.

12th September – The Duke of Gloucester came to stay with Her Royal Highness and on the following Monday the Queen came for a week. They both look very nice. They visited Harrogate on Tuesday 15th September, Castle Howard Wednesday, High Harrogate Thursday, Ripon etc Friday, York on Saturday and on Sunday the Queen attended morning service. The church was packed and a great number had to stay outside. The Queen and Princess Mary looked beautiful, so did Lord Harewood and their two charming sons. In the afternoon Her Majesty and Her Royal Highness went to Bramham. The Queen left for Balmoral early on Monday morning. I went to the corner to see her off – 21st September 1931.

Homely Royal Visit – The Queen's week at Harewood
When the Queen comes to Harewood on Monday for her week's stay with Princess Mary and the Earl of Harewood at Harewood House, there will be no alteration in the quiet, old-world atmosphere which this village possesses, although it is only a few miles from the industrial centres of the West Riding.

Everything is being done to keep the Queen's visit a quiet and homely family gathering. "Its just like any other mother coming to see how her daughter has settled down in her new home. We know that, so there will be no fuss", one of the villagers told me today.

Gay welcome to the Queen – visit to Princess Mary
When the Queen drove from Harrogate to Harewood this evening on her way to the home of Princess Mary and the Earl of Harewood at Harewood House, where she is to stay for a week, motorists who had parked their cars in the country lanes off the main road lined the road to cheer her as she drove by. Motorists had driven in from all parts of Yorkshire to give this welcome to the Queen, who smiled and bowed her acknowledgements. All along the road from Harrogate to Harewood there were cheering groups of people, while in the little grey village itself, all the villagers had gathered along the street and by the gates to Harewood Park to welcome the Queen. Here also were large numbers of people who had come by motor car, and lines of cars were parked along the

road leading to Harewood Avenue, the fine avenue of trees which leads to the village.

At the gates of the park Mr J Ibbotson, one of the oldest servants on the Estate, was standing to attention as the Queen passed, and village children joined in the cheering. The villagers are hoping that the Queen will follow an old custom of visitors to Harewood and plant a tree in a corner of the grounds near the church. I understand that it is very possible that the Queen will do this during her stay.

It is anticipated that there will be a big congregation on Sunday morning at the little church of Harewood, which stands in the edge of the park, for it is expected that the Queen, Princess Mary and the Earl of Harewood, and the Queen's two grandsons will attend the morning service.

The Queen at Church
The Queen, with Princess Mary and the Earl of Harewood and their two sons, yesterday morning attended service at the church of Harewood, which is a few minutes walk from Harewood House. Every seat in the church was filled, for besides the villagers and tenants, visitors had come by motorcar from a large area round about. Seats were reserved for the village people and for tenants. Cars were parked all along the tree lined lane leading from the village to the church. Seated almost opposite the royal family were Girl Guides and Brownies of the Harewood Troop in which Princess Mary takes a keen interest. It was a simple service in the simple grey old country church set among the trees of the park.

Happy boy and the Queen – a treat for the scholars (Friday)
The Queen gave the children of the little village school of Harewood a happy surprise when shortly after they had begun their afternoon lessons today it was announced that her car would stop at the gates of the park so that they might see her. All the scholars have been greatly excited over the Queen's visit to Harewood – but very few of them had seen her, because when she has driven out of the park most of them have been in school. So the Queen arranged today that they should assemble at the gates as she drove out on her way to Ripon. All the children marched to the gates and lined up on the green lawn beside the lodge. The car was stopped here while the Queen spoke for a few minutes to Mr J H Wadsworth, the schoolmaster. One of the youngest scholars, Kenneth Nicholson, aged four, is certain that the Queen smiled at him. "I've seen the real Queen" he told me excitedly after school today. "I saw her ever so well just in front of me".

Later the Queen visited some of the tenants' houses near the stables. Harewood, with its quaint grey cottages set in green backwaters off the main road, is at its best for the Queen's visit. The high trees which surround the village are showing the first tinges of brown and blue. Wood smoke curls up against them from the cottage chimneys.

Court and Society
The Queen, who has actively enjoyed her stay with Princess Mary at Harewood House, returns to Balmoral, according to present arrangements on Monday. The Queen spent yesterday morning going through Harewood House in company with Princess Mary in order to inspect the redecoration of the Princess's home. After lunch she walked in the gardens with her two grandsons and the Duke of Gloucester. Her Majesty intends to make a complete tour of the Harewood Estate, home farm, and stud headquarters, and on Sunday she will attend morning service at the twelfth-century church within the estate grounds.

Princess Mary's two sons were at church on Sunday 27th September.

Princess Mary and Lord Harewood have been staying in London for a time. Princess Mary came home on Monday 9th November. HRH attended her first meet on Wednesday at Creskeld Hall where she joined in the two minutes silence.

On Saturday afternoon, 14th November 1931, Her Royal Highness presented badges to the First Harewood Brownie Pack. The Brownies gave the grand Howl to welcome Her Royal Highness. The smallest Brownie presented Princess Mary with a bouquet. There were many things for Princess Mary to see – the Fairy Ring, Inspection, presentation of badges, etc. Afterwards tea was served and at 5.00pm all came to an end after two hours of enjoyment.

On Sunday 15th November, Princess Mary and her two sons attended morning service.

On Sunday 22nd November, HRH Princess Mary attended morning service with Lord Harewood, Lord Lascelles and Master Gerald. Lord Harewood read the lessons.

Her Royal Highness and Lord Harewood attended the meet on Wednesday 25th November. I met them coming back as I was coming up the park.

Princess Mary and Lord Harewood entertained a large house party for shooting. The Duke and Duchess of York were among the guests – December 1931.

Princess Mary, Lord Lascelles and the Hon Gerald, attended Bertram Mills Circus with Mr N Fitzroy, Estate Agent. The two boys enjoyed it very much.

The Princess and the blind girl – pretty incident at Harewood
When Princess Mary paid a visit to the Old Hall Farm, Pontefract, which is in the Harewood Estate, she was told that living on the farm was a little blind girl, Iris Simpson, who would love it if she would look in to see her. At once Princess Mary consented and had a long talk with the girl, who timidly asked if she would accept a basket she had made. To her delight the Princess said she would be very pleased to take it.

Her Royal Highness presented prizes at Harewood School on Monday 21st December. She walked up to the school.

Princess Mary and Lord Harewood entertained a large house party for Christmas.

Christmas with the Royal Babies
Princess Elizabeth is being taught the joy of giving at Christmas and Lord Lascelles and his brother Gerald were early and apt pupils in the delight of it. Princess Mary still keeps the nurseries at Chesterfield House, and they are beautifully light and airy rooms, with many glass-fronted cupboards, where the Lascelles boys keep their toys, chiefly mechanical ones.

The nurseries at Harewood House are known as "the playrooms" now, and as Lord Lascelles and his brother Gerald are so often with their parents, they are not used a great deal. These playrooms are large, airy and practical, as boys' rooms should be – and Princess Mary understands what boys need better than anyone else, almost.

Lord Lascelles and his brother Gerald – even if they actually spend Christmas at Sandringham – first sing carols with the village children, and enjoy the lighted Christmas tree in the village schoolroom at their Yorkshire home. They have simple tastes, and enjoy this event just as eagerly as do the other children.

Last Christmas, Princess Mary and Lord Harewood did not go to Sandringham, but stayed at Harewood House, so Princess Mary gave a party for her sons in the oak-panelled library at Harewood House, and about a dozen of their little friends, with a conjuror and a Christmas tree to amuse them all. Princess Mary organised the games, and the children enjoyed themselves immensely – not the less because their hostess played with them herself.

On 31st December 1931, HRH Princess Mary and Lord Harewood attended the Christmas tea for the elder people of Harewood given by members of the Women's Institute. Her Royal Highness cut the cake, both she and Lord Harewood pulled crackers and wore the fancy paper caps. After the tea there were games etc. Princess Mary was the winner in the game of musical parcel but handed her prize to Mrs Watkinson – which was a pound of tea. After a very enjoyable evening, Her Royal Highness and Lord Harewood left the school for their dinner at Harewood House.

1932

On 1st January 1932, Her Royal Highness Princess Mary, Countess of Harewood, took the title of the Princess Royal. The title had previously been held by the King's sister until she died on 4th January 1931. May she live many years to hold that title. I wish her every happiness and success.

> *Title of Princess Royal*
> *Under the New Year Honours announced last night, Princess Mary will bear the title of Princess Royal. In a special supplement to the London Gazette appeared the announcement:-*
>
> *The King has been graciously pleased to declare that His Majesty's daughter, Her Royal Highness Princess Victoria Alexandra Alice Mary (Countess of Harewood) shall henceforth bear the style and title of Princess Royal, January 1st 1932.*
>
> *The honour bestowed upon Princess Mary will be warmly welcomed particularly in the North where, since her marriage to Lord Harewood, then Viscount Lascelles, in 1922, she has spent most of her time.*

6th January – Her Royal Highness and Lord Harewood left Harewood to go to London to see their new house in Green Street, a present from the Queen.

Lord Lascelles and Master Gerald attended church on Sunday 10th January.

The Princess Royal and Lord Harewood arrived home from London on 12th January.

The Princess Royal and Lord Harewood attended church on Sunday 17th January. Lord Harewood read the lessons. The Princess looked beautiful in her strawberry outfit.

On Friday 11th March 1932, the Women's Institute had the pleasure of entertaining Her Royal Highness. She was with us about an hour and a half. We had to stand before her and other members of the Institute advertising foods. I was Brown & Polson's cornflour. There were about 18 of us. I think Her Royal Highness and all enjoyed themselves.

Princess Royal, Lord Harewood and Lord Lascelles attended the Bramham Moor Point to Point on Saturday 9th April, near Swindon Wood, about 3 miles from Harewood. Five races were run in all, after which Her Royal Highness presented cups.

On Monday 11th April, Her Royal Highness and Lord Harewood left for London.

19th March – The Princess Royal was in Leeds with Lord Middleton and the Lord Mayor of Leeds to open the Brotherton House headquarters of Toc H.

Wednesday 20th April 1932 – Her Royal Highness presented the Haig Cup at the British Legion Conference in London.

25th April – Her Royal Highness was 35 years old – I wish her many happy returns.

Lord Lascelles, Princess Royal's eldest son, started school on 5th May 1932 at Ludgrove School, Cockfosters, Middlesex.

Princess Royal and Lord Harewood are staying in London for the season.

Princess Royal and Lord Harewood arrived home from London on Friday 20th May. On Sunday 22nd, she presented flags to the First Harewood Boy Scouts. The Princess Royal attended church in her Guide uniform.

Her Royal Highness and Lord Harewood are opening Harewood House to the public on Wednesdays and Thursdays in aid of charity. It was open for the first time on 12th May. It was also open on Whit Monday and the money then was in aid of a village hall for Harewood – they took just over £500.

May 21st – The Princess inspected members of the North Riding Red Cross Society at Thirsk.

Princess Royal came home accompanied by Lord Harewood for the York race meeting, both looked very nice when passing for the races on Tuesday 24th May.

Her Royal Highness and Lord Harewood have been staying in London for Ascot week.

The Princess Royal and Lord Harewood have kindly lent Harewood House for the Women's Institute of Yorkshire Singing and Dancing Competition, 25th and 26th June 1932.

Her Royal Highness and Lord Harewood arrived home from London on Monday 4th July. On Wednesday 6th July, the Princess Royal received the Freedom of the City of Leeds.

The Princess Royal, Lord Harewood and their two sons arrived home on Friday 29th July for the rest of the summer. On Saturday 30th, Her Royal Highness presented prizes at the Bramham Moor Hunt puppy walk at Hope Hall, Bramham near Tadcaster. Lord Lascelles was also there. Lord Harewood attended the Yorkshire British Legion Rally. On Sunday Princess Royal, Lord Harewood and their two sons attended morning service.

Thursday 4th August – Her Royal Highness inspected nurses on her arrival to the new Skipton and District Hospital.

Saturday 6th August – The Princess Royal opened the Harewood Village Fete in the grounds of Harewood vicarage. She watched the Harewood Brownies May-Pole dance and visited the stalls. The weather was beautiful all day.

> *Happy Fete at Harewood – Visit by the Princess Royal – Her wait at the gate*
> *The Princess Royal had a novel experience today. She had promised to open a garden fete held in the grounds of Harewood vicarage in aid of the village hall, the First Harewood (Princess Royal's Own) Brownie Pack and the First Harewood Wolf Cub Pack. The vicarage stands on the edge of the Park and it was expected that the Princess Royal would drive from Harewood House to the main gate of the vicarage. The organisers were standing on the steps of the vicarage awaiting her arrival, but the Princess decided to walk across the park with her lady-in-waiting, Miss Sybil Kenyon-Slaney, to a side gate. Arriving there she found it locked, and had to wait outside. Some time elapsed before her presence there was discovered and the gate was unlocked for her to walk into the vicarage grounds.*
>
> *The Princess Royal takes a keen interest in the Harewood Brownies and Wolf Cubs. The whole affair was conducted in a jolly, informal atmosphere. The Princess Royal had filled one of the stalls with her own gifts, and she spent a*

long time visiting the stalls and chatting with the attendants.

She had tea in the vicarage, and afterwards watched a display of Morris and May-Pole dancing and plays given by the local Brownies and Wolf Cubs who, incidentally, gave the Princess Royal a vigorous 'Howl' of welcome.

The Brownies' Fete
As a rule, garden fetes which are opened by Royalty are very grand affairs with elaborate arrangements and half the county there to do the honours. The fete which the Princess Royal opened in the vicarage gardens at Harewood on Saturday afternoon was on a different plane altogether. It was a small, informal affair to which the Princess went because of her interest in all things connected with the village of Harewood. Since the fete was organised by the Princess Royal's Own Brownie pack and the 1st Harewood Wolf Cubs, the Princess had a special interest in it.

The little incident which marked the Princess's arrival seemed to amuse her as much as it did the crowd. Being a fine sunny afternoon the Princess had decided to walk across the Park to the vicarage instead of driving there, with the result that she found herself locked out. All eyes were on the drive, expecting every moment to see the royal car appear, and it was some minutes before it was realised that the Princess and her lady-in-waiting were standing outside waiting for the gate to be unlocked.

For the short opening ceremony the Princess stood on the steps of the vicarage with the Guides, Brownies and Cubs formed up in front of her and the visitors seated in a semi-circle round.

Afterwards the Princess went round the stalls. The gifts sent by the Princess had been set apart and these were quickly bought up.

Everyone was delighted to find that the Princess had no intention of leaving early. After the semi-official tour of the stalls with the vicar, the Rev H H Griffith, the Princess sat with some of the Guide officers and watched the dancing display on the lawn, going in to the vicarage to tea and coming out again for the second half of the programme. Several of the Guides the Princess had met before and with these she talked for a long time. Many of the Brownies, too, the Princess knew by sight and her acknowledgement of their salutes was a very friendly smile.

19th August – The Princess Royal opened our Women's Institute Flower Show. She presented the prizes and also shook hands with each winner.

Margaret won First Prize for the best jelly. Princess Royal and Lord Lascelles were keen bidders while the sale was on.

Saturday 20th August – The King and Queen arrived at Harewood about 5.45pm. There was a great crowd to welcome them. I saw them both, they looked very nice. It started to rain then and didn't stop until the Royal Party left on Monday.

> *The King at Harewood – His Grandson's birthday – Royal party in the playroom*
> *When the King and Queen visit Harewood House, the home of the Princess Royal and the Earl of Harewood, on Saturday there will arrive, it is very probable, several mysterious looking packages, birthday presents for the younger grandson of the King and Queen, the Hon Gerald Lascelles, who will be eight years old on Sunday. The birthdays of the two sons of the Princess Royal are generally celebrated by a family tea party in the playrooms on the top storey of Harewood House, which have a view over a large part of the park. It is expected that the King and Queen will this year attend this happy little gathering of members of the family and take part in the tea-party, which usually includes special party dishes which would appeal to any boy.*
>
> *The weekend visit of the King and Queen to the home of their daughter will be a very quiet one. It is expected that most of the time will be spent in the grounds of the park, where tree-lined avenues are now in the full beauty of summer.*
>
> *This is the first visit the King has paid to Harewood House since it became the home of the Princess Royal, and besides seeing the re-arrangement of the House which was carried out under the supervision of the Princess, the King and Queen will, it is expected, spend much time in the terraced gardens, which contain most of the Princess's favourite flowers, and which stand above the woods and lake of the park.*
>
> *The royal party will attend the service at the village church at Harewood on Sunday morning. Seats have been allotted to the villagers in the centre of this church, and it is not expected that this old grey church, which for all the modern electric lighting which has been installed is still typical of the ivy-covered village churches of this part of Yorkshire, will accommodate all the visitors who wish to attend the service. The royal party will arrive by the private entrance to the church across the park from the House. Afterwards the King and Queen will follow the old Harewood tradition of planting a tree in the grounds to commemorate their visit.*

Royal visit to Harewood House – King and Queen's stay with Princess Royal

When the King and Queen arrive at Harrogate shortly before 5.30pm today for their weekend's stay with the Earl of Harewood and the Princess Royal at Harewood House, they will step from the royal train on to a platform which has been transformed into a flower garden. Banks of flowers have been placed on the arrival platform, and when they walk to their car for the short journey to Harewood, the King and Queen will pass under an archway of roses.

During their journey the King and Queen will see views over the moors to the west of Harewood and the ruined Castle in the grounds of the House shortly before they reach the village which is preparing to give them a loyal welcome.

The Queen cuts grandson's birthday cake – Happy Royal tea party – Boy Viscount deputises for the King

Unceasing rain today sadly interfered with the out-of-doors programme of the King and Queen, who are on a brief visit here to the Princess Royal and the Earl of Harewood; but as their Majesties were kept indoors, except that they attended the morning service at Harewood Church, the birthday celebrations of the Hon Gerald Lascelles, the younger son of the Princess Royal and Lord Harewood, who was eight today, received all the more attention from his grandparents. At a merry birthday tea party this afternoon, the Queen cut a splendid iced cake made specially for the occasion.

The Hon Gerald and his elder brother, Viscount Lascelles, were also called upon to deputise for the King and Queen in planting cedar of Lebanon trees in the park this afternoon in memory of the visit. Viscount Lascelles planted a tree on behalf of the King, and the Hon Gerald was deputy for the Queen.

Accompanying the King and Queen at the church service this morning were the Princess Royal and Lord Harewood, with the two boys, and Lord and Lady Boyne's daughter Rosemary, who is on a visit to Harewood.

It was raining so heavily that they came across the park in motorcars to the church door. Although the weather was so bad the old church, which seats about 500, was well filled ... almost everyone in the village must have been present, all the pews in the centre aisles, which were reserved for Harewood residents, were packed.

On Saturday 3rd September, the Bramham Moor Hunt held their Gymkhana in Harewood Park. Lord Lascelles and the Hon Gerald, were keen competitors. Her Royal Highness was one of the judges and graciously distributed the prizes at the end of the afternoon. The band played God Save the King, and all came to an end.

Bob-Apple Racing
The keenest competitors at the Bramham Moor Hunt Gymkhana on Saturday were, I am told, the sons of the Princess Royal and Lord Harewood. Young Lord Lascelles, the elder of the two … went in for a bob-apple competition, in which his determination fired the imagination of the crowd that was watching. Time after time he plunged his face and head into a tin bucket of water and sought to secure an apple with his teeth, but he was overcome with laughter – as were his parents who were watching him – and by the time he succeeded in seizing the apple his chance of winning had slipped by.

On Sunday 4th September, the Princess Royal, Lord Harewood and the Dowager Countess of Harewood, attended morning service. Lord Lascelles and the Hon Gerald were also there. Lord Harewood read the lessons. Her Royal Highness was in grey with a black fur.

On Monday 5th September, Her Royal Highness and Lord Harewood left to join Lord Lonsdale's house party for the St Leger, returning home on Friday 9th September (Lord Harewood celebrated his birthday).

Her Royal Highness and Lord Harewood entertained a large number of children from the Hunt in Harewood park on Saturday 10th September. The Earl and Countess Athlone were with Lord Harewood and Her Royal Highness.

Princess Royal and Lord Harewood accompanied by their two sons and the Earl and Countess of Athlone attended church. Lord Harewood read the lessons. Princess Royal was dressed in black.

Her Royal Highness attended by Miss Yorke, her lady-in-waiting, attended the Horticultural Show which was held in the Winter Gardens, Harrogate, on Thursday 15th September.

A flutter at the flower show
The news received late last night that the Princess Royal intended to pay a private visit to the flower show at the Winter Gardens, Harrogate today, threw exhibitors and officials into a flutter. Some guessed that the Princess plans to start a water-garden at Harewood soon for she was particularly interested in suitable plants and took a great fancy to a little scarlet flower which grows near water, discussing its possibilities at length with her gardener.

Hospital Contrasts
On Saturday the Princess will visit Harrogate again to open the new General
Hospital. It is indeed a wonderful sight ... the low, wide walls seem made of
windows. In imagination one sees the wind blowing through the building
carrying away all ills.

Thursday 22nd September – Lord Lascelles went back to school.

Sunday 25th September – Her Royal Highness and Lord Harewood attended
morning service accompanied by the Hon Gerald. Lord Harewood read the
lessons. The Princess looked beautiful in a grey coat with brown fur collar
and a red hat.

Sunday 2nd October – The Princess Royal and Lord Harewood attended
morning service. Lord Harewood read the lessons.

Monday 3rd October – Her Royal Highness presented the prizes at the close
of the annual Harewood Feast sports. She looked beautiful in grey.

Tuesday 4th October – Her Royal Highness attended the Women's Institute.
She arrived prompt at 7 o'clock, listened to the lecture given by Dr Barr,
watched the dancing, joined in the competition. Margaret was the winner.
Her Royal Highness presented the prizes.

Lord Harewood arrived home from London on Friday 28th October. He
attended morning service on Sunday morning and read the lessons.

Her Royal Highness and Lord Harewood attended morning service on
Sunday 6th November. Lord Harewood read the lessons. The Princess was
dressed in a beautiful fur coat. In the afternoon, Her Royal Highness and
Lord Harewood went to an Armistice service. Lord Harewood made a
speech on war etc.

On Friday 18th November, the Women's Institute held their fancy dress, at
which the Princess Royal was judge. Many things amused the Princess. She
looked beautiful in a long green dress, green shoes, coat and a beautiful
necklace. The Princess also judged many dances. After about an hour and a
half, the Princess left for Harewood House.

Saturday 19th November, Her Royal Highness went hunting in the morning,
then in the afternoon she presented prizes at the Harewood Barracks, Leeds
(61st Detachment Barnsley VAD).

Sunday 4th December – The Princess Royal attended church with the Hon Gerald.

The Princess Royal left Harewood for London on Wednesday 7th December to do her Christmas shopping. The Princess Royal and Lord Harewood arrived back from London on Friday 16th December.

The Princess Royal presented prizes at Harewood School on Tuesday 20th December, then went to East Keswick at night.

On Christmas Day, the Princess Royal and Lord Harewood attended 8 o'clock communion with a number of the house party then again attended the morning service with a larger number of the house party. The Princess looked beautiful.

From 'Red Indians' to 'Eskimos' – the Princess Royal's sons want snow

The old-world village of Harewood is a typical setting for an old-fashioned Christmas, and that is the sort that will be celebrated at Harewood House by the Princess Royal, Lord Harewood and their two sons. The house party, which will include the Dowager Countess of Harewood, Major and Mrs Edward Lascelles, and Lord and Lady Boyne, will attend service on Sunday morning in Harewood church.

The Princess Royal herself distributed presents at a party for the village children, and devoted a whole day to sending out parcels of toys to children whom she has visited in hospitals in many centres of Yorkshire.

Lord Lascelles, who returned home from school a few days ago, and his younger brother are considering a change from Red Indians to Eskimos. During the summer the hut wigwam which they built themselves on the banks of the lake has been the headquarters of two chiefs of a large band of Indians who wrote on birch bark and occasionally ambushed gardeners. This has now been covered by the boys with a roof and walls of fir branches, and only snow is needed to turn it into an ideal igloo. But the suggestion by one of the Princess Royal's sons that hardy Eskimos should really sleep out in a snow-bound home have not, I understand, met with entire approval.

On Friday 30th December, the Princess Royal accompanied by Miss Kenyon-Slaney, came to the Christmas party which is given by the Women's Institute to the older people of this parish. The Princess arrived prompt at 4.30pm and received a grand welcome. Her Royal Highness cut the cake and tea was begun. After tea many games were played and at 6 o'clock a concert was given by members of the Women's Institute. The Princess stayed until 7.30pm when she left for Harewood House.

1933

On 1st January 1933, the Princess Royal and Lord Harewood, accompanied by Lord Lascelles and Master Gerald, attended morning service.

On Saturday 14th January 1933, the 1st Harewood (Princess Royal's Own) Brownie Pack held their annual presentation of badges and service stars. HRH the Princess Royal graciously consented to present them. A number of invitations were issued and many officials and Brown Owls attended. The Princess arrived prompt at 3pm. The Brownies gave a Grand Howl to welcome her. After this, she presented badges. On me was conferred the honour of handing the badges to the Princess. After the presentation of badges, etc, I was enrolled as Speckled Owl of the pack by Her Royal Highness. She then shook hands with me. After this, there was a demonstration of Brownie Badge work, the Brownies sang songs and played games, then the 1st Harewood Guides served tea to the Princess, the Guide Officials and the visitors. After tea the Brownies gave a most interesting play entitled 'the road to Bethlehem' which the Princess like everyone else apparently enjoyed immensely. Then the visiting Guide Officials were introduced to HRH. At 5.20pm the Princess left, after assuring the Brown Owl that she had thoroughly enjoyed herself.

Prince George arrived at Harewood on Saturday afternoon (14th January) for the weekend and left on Monday morning.

15th January – Her Royal Highness attended church accompanied by Lord Lascelles and the Hon Gerald.

The Princess Royal and Lord Harewood spent a great deal of time skating on the lake during the third week in January. Ice hockey was played quite a number of times. Her Royal Highness and Lord Harewood are beautiful skaters.

Saturday 4th February – Her Royal Highness attended the meet of the Bramham Moor Hunt at Wood Hall Bridge, accompanied by the Hon Gerald. There were a large number of followers, both mounted and on foot.

When the Princess Royal attended church on Sunday 5th February, she was dressed in black, owing to the death of her aunt, Lady Slaney.

Sunday 12th February – The Princess Royal attended morning service accompanied by Prince George, Lord Harewood and the Hon Gerald, also Miss Vigers the Governess.

19th February – The Princess Royal and Lord Harewood attended morning service accompanied by the Hon Gerald.

Monday 20th February – Her Royal Highness left for Buckingham Palace.

Sunday 26th February – The Princess Royal attended morning service with Lord Harewood. The weather was simply terrible. The congregation numbered only six. His Lordship read the lessons. I think a few more should follow Her Royal Highness's example by turning out whatever weather for church.

Sunday 5th March – The Princess Royal and Lord Harewood attended morning service accompanied by the Hon Gerald.

> ### Princess without a penny – Lord Harewood's loan
> *There was not as numerous an attendance as usual, either of followers or the general public, this morning at the meet of the Bramham Moor Hunt in Harewood village. After effects of the big storm are still such that there are still large tracts of the country closed to the Hunt by flooding or snow and accordingly the venue was changed to Harewood village.*
>
> *Today's meet was the occasion for the annual "Cap" for the Hunt Servants' Benefit Society – an organisation which exists to help hunt servants and their dependents who fall on bad times. The Princess Royal had evidently overlooked the fact that the "Cap" was to be sent round and when the collector approached her she had to confess with dismay she had no money – but Lord Harewood saved the situation. "I'll give a pound for you" he said, and duly obliged, laughingly remarking to the Princess, "That's a pound you owe me".*

Her Royal Highness attended morning service accompanied by Lord Harewood, the Hon Gerald and Lady Boyne's daughter, Rosemary, on 12th March.

Sunday 19th March – The Princess Royal, accompanied by his Lordship and Master Gerald, attended morning service. All looked charming.

On Thursday the Princess Royal received purses at Leeds Town Hall on behalf of the Waifs and Strays in Yorkshire. There was a large gathering.

Sunday 2nd April – The Princess Royal, accompanied by Princess Helen Victoria, Lord Harewood and Master Gerald, also Miss Yorke and Miss Vigers, attended morning service. Lord Harewood read the lessons. In the afternoon, Her Royal Highness left for London. She arrived home from London on Tuesday 4th April.

On Tuesday evening, 4th April, the Princess Royal attended the Women's Institute meeting. Her Royal Highness was received by Mrs Oldfield. The Princess was in the chair for business then all watched the lecture of how to make salads and at about 8.30pm the Princess left.

On Saturday 8th April, the Princess Royal attended the Bramham Moor Hunt point-to-point accompanied by Lord Harewood, the Dowager Lady Harewood, Lord Lascelles and the Hon Gerald. At the close of the race meeting, Her Royal Highness presented cups.

The Princess Royal, Lord Harewood and their two sons, left Harewood on Thursday for Windsor Castle. They attended many things whilst away from Harewood – Aldershot, the races, and many other exciting events including Princess Elizabeth's birthday party. The Princess Royal celebrated her 36th birthday while on her stay in London.

Her Royal Highness and Lord Harewood arrived at Harewood from London on Saturday 15th May, for York races.

The Princess Royal and Lord Harewood attended church on Sunday morning, 16th May. Her Royal Highness looked beautiful in a green costume with a lovely fur. Lord Harewood read the lessons.

The Princess and Lord Harewood went to York races on Tuesday, Wednesday and Thursday, the first two days accompanied by Mr and Miss Clayton. On Friday, Her Royal Highness left for London.

Her Royal Highness and Lord Harewood arrived home on Saturday after seeing the Changing of the Guards for His Majesty's birthday.

Her Royal Highness and Lord Harewood attended early service on Whit Sunday. On Monday the Princess was quite busy in the pleasure grounds. The Princess Royal and Lord Harewood left for London on Tuesday 5th June.

The Princess Royal had a very busy time in May and June including engagements in Manchester, Lancaster, Brentwood, Oswestry, Shrewsbury, Liverpool, Derby, Edinburgh and London. On 5th July, according to the newspapers, she has to rest for a while. On 19th July, Her Royal Highness returned home from London for a rest owing to a very bad break-down.

On Thursday 10th August, Lord Lascelles and the Hon Gerald attended the Women's Institute flower show and both were keen. They were accompanied by Miss Kenyon-Slaney, Miss Bliss and Miss Vigers.

The King and Queen arrived at Harewood on 21st August, about 5.30pm. Hundreds of people gathered to welcome them. Prince George also came.

The King and Queen, accompanied by the Princess Royal and Lord Harewood, went round the stud farm and gardens. Prince George also went with them – Tuesday 22nd August. The Queen attended morning service.

Her Royal Highness is much better now. She attended morning service on Sunday 8th October and left for Newmarket on 9th October.

The Princess Royal – operation for appendicitis – her condition satisfactory

The Princess Royal, only daughter of the King and Queen, is suffering from appendicitis. The following bulletin was issued: "The Princess Royal underwent an operation this morning for the removal of the appendix. Her Royal Highness is so far doing well." (7th November 1933). The following bulletin was issued last night, "The Princess Royal has passed a fairly comfortable day and her condition is satisfactory."

For many years until the middle of the Summer, the Princess Royal was one of the busiest members of the Royal Family. Her record of public engagements almost equalled that of the Prince of Wales. Then the strain told. In August she was compelled to cancel all her engagements and to rest at Harewood House, her Yorkshire home. Her doctors forbade her to take part in any function or ceremony until the end of September or October. Her husband, the Earl of Harewood, announced that she was "extremely indisposed" and had greatly overtaxed her strength during the Summer.

The Queen comforts her daughter

This is the human story behind the operation on the Princess Royal. The Princess drove to Buckingham Palace last Sunday to see her mother. The Queen knew that for months the Princess Royal had been fighting against ill-health. The news that she had appendicitis had upset her. She talked quietly to her daughter; soothed her fears. The Princess Royal drove back to her Mayfair home contented, to prepare for the operation. She had insisted that no one beside the King should be told.

The Princess Royal had been in failing health since early Summer. She lost two stones in weight in four months, but now she is making excellent progress. She will probably spend a fortnight's convalescence in a south coast resort before returning to her Yorkshire home at Harewood House to complete her recovery.

All the people of Harewood were delighted when news came of Her Royal Highness's successful operation.

Village's relief – anxious wait for news
Today I was able to tell the cheering news to Harewood, the Yorkshire home of the Princess Royal, that the Princess was progressing favourably following her operation. The whole of the village had been anxiously awaiting news.

Since she came to Harewood the Princess Royal has taken a keen personal interest in all the activities of the village. "The Princess is very much our own and has mixed with us a great deal" said a village woman. "Some of our happiest gatherings have been at the monthly Women's Institute meetings, over which the Princess nearly always presides when she is in residence here".

No bulletins were posted on the gates of the grounds of Harewood House, but the news travelled quickly round the village. Farmers from distant corners of the Estate came into the village this afternoon to learn the latest tidings.

1934
The Princess Royal left Harewood on 22nd February for a two month tour round Tangiers etc. They arrived back for Easter.

Operation on Viscount Lascelles – an abscess on the neck (March 1934)

Viscount Lascelles, the elder son of the Princess Royal and the Earl of Harewood, underwent an operation in London today for an abscess on the neck. The operation was performed in a London nursing home. Immediately afterwards, the King and Queen were informed of the result and messages were sent to the Princess Royal and the Earl of Harewood who are abroad to complete her convalescence after an operation for appendicitis last November.

Viscount Lascelles is a good football player, an excellent shot with a miniature rifle and a great lover of horses. Swimming is another of his recreations. At school geography is one of his favourite subjects. He is a great reader, particularly of books on motor cars or engines. At Harewood House he has a library of his own, containing many books of this type. An unusual accomplishment which Viscount Lascelles possesses is the ability to knit and a scarlet wool muffler made by him was contributed to an exhibition of Queen Mary's London Needlework Guild.

The Princess Royal celebrated her 38th birthday at Harewood House on 25th April 1934.

Princess Royal's birthday – celebration at Windsor

The birthday of the Princess Royal was celebrated at Windsor yesterday. The bells of St George's Chapel and of Windsor Parish Church were rung and flags flown on public buildings. The Princess Royal spent her birthday quietly at Harewood House, her Yorkshire home, where she and the Earl of Harewood have been in residence since they returned at Easter from their visit to Palestine and Rome. Her two sons, Viscount Lascelles and the Hon Gerald Lascelles, were with the Princess.

Surprise for the Princess Royal's Son – Bat from the Australians

The King's grandson, Viscount Lascelles (elder son of the Princess Royal and the Earl of Harewood) must have gone to bed last night with an extra helping of youthful contentment. The eleven years old lad had learned that a wish very near to his heart was coming true. He is very keen on cricket and is taking a great interest in the visit of the Australians. He knows records, for he is a diligent student of "Wisden" and other cricket literature. The thought came to him that perhaps he might get the Australian team to put their autographs on his bat. Hearing of the boy's interest in them, the Australians have anticipated his wish. They are presenting him with a special bat in commemoration of their visit. It will bear all their autographs and will be sent to him within the next day or so at the Princess Royal's home in London. The King is aware of his grandson's devotion to cricket and also of this kindly gesture of the Australians.

The Queen arrived at Harewood on Monday 20th August at 6.30pm. While on her stay here she visited many places, always accompanied by the Princess Royal. On Sunday 27th, the Queen, Princess Royal and Lord Lascelles, attended morning service and all looked beautiful. The Queen went to Bramham in the afternoon and on Monday morning left for Scotland.

The Princess Royal and Lord Harewood entertained a large house party for York Races.

On Saturday 1st September 1934, the Princess Royal opened our garden fete – in aid of the 1st Harewood (Princess Royal's Own) Brownies. She arrived at the vicarage at 3pm met by Brown Owl and the Vicar. When she arrived at the steps she shook hands with us all. The Brownies gave a Pack Howl and presented a bouquet. The Vicar made a speech then the Princess declared the fete open. She made a tour of the stalls and side shows then sat and watched dancing by the Brownies. The Princess had tea at the vicarage then at 5 o'clock left for Harrogate where she presented prizes at the Gymkhana. The Princess bought the bag which Margaret had made.

Princess Royal with her Brownies at Harewood
The Princess Royal spent nearly 2 hours in the grounds of Harewood vicarage on Saturday with her own pack of Brownies. She was there officially to open the fete held annually by the Pack, the 1st Harewood (the Princess Royal's Own) Brownies. Last year she was unable to attend because of her illness. The Princess, accompanied by Miss Kenyon-Slaney, walked round the stalls and side-shows and bought a number of articles. About 500 people attended the fete and there was keen competition for the Princess Royal's gifts which were on sale at one of the stalls.

On Monday 10th September, the Princess Royal and Lord Harewood left for Doncaster. They were the guests of Lord and Lady Lonsdale. All attended the race meetings for three days then on Friday 14th September the Princess and Lord Harewood left for home.

The Princess Royal and Lord Harewood accompanied by Lord Lascelles and the Hon Gerald attended morning service on Sunday 16th September.

On 25th September, the Princess Royal unveiled a bust of His Majesty the King at the Civic Hall, Leeds.

On Sunday 30th September the Princess Royal accompanied by Princess Helen Victoria and Lord Harewood attended morning service.

On Monday 1st October, Her Royal Highness presented the prizes at the close of the Feast sports. She also judged the children's pet section.

After the entry above, and a few pages of newspaper cuttings, nothing else was written in Olive's book until she wrote the poem below following the death of The Princess Royal in 1965. So, for 31 years Olive's book remained untouched. Why? We will never know. One thing is very clear, the poem, and all that was written in Olive's book prior to that, is an indication of just how much affection, admiration and love, Olive felt for 'her' Princess Royal.

A Real Lady
Olive Wild

In a garden sweet and fair
Once a Lady lingered there
Now that she has passed away
Her thoughts still in that garden lay

She tended it with loving care
The flowers bloomed so well
She watered them, did not despair
Oh what a glorious smell

The blooms they lasted for so long
The sun shone every day
The birds would sing their little song
Amongst the flowers so gay

The flowers then began to die
When autumn came along
And we began to wonder why
The birds left out their song

The Lady who would tend the soil
Was always good and kind
We knew her as The Princess Royal
No better could you find

Those who knew her very well
Loved her nationwide
Sadness upon Harewood fell
The day that Lady died

CHAPTER NINE
Harewood Fond Memories

Views of Harewood on a Postcard

© W Bramley, Publisher The Electric Printing Works, Crossgates, Leeds
Postcard kindly provided by John Newby

Introduction

The stories below are from a variety of people. Interestingly, most of them were given to me by women and many of the 'authors' are at least sixty years old. So, where did the stories come from?

Firstly, many months ago I hand-delivered letters to everyone in the village that I knew had been living in the village ten or more years and therefore might have a story or two to tell. Secondly, in early 2007 I put a small 'request for help' piece in the Parish magazine in order to find others, who might not live in Harewood but who might have stories to tell. Some people wished to be interviewed, rather than to write their stories down, so I had

149

one to one meetings with a number of people as well. Whilst the stories below contain the exact words of the 'story teller', the titles for each story were created by me.

A number of the memories are about the village itself, a few are about Harewood House and many pertain to memories of members of the Royal Family, especially The Princess Royal. Some are very personal recollections. Many evoke wonderful memories of a bygone era and give a real feel for the village community and a way of life which sadly no longer exists today. I am very grateful to everyone who contributed to this Chapter of memories.

A Youthful Idyll

My childhood memories go back over 50 years to days spent playing cowboys and Indians in the woods with the other boys and we had our own 'Rocky Mountains' – which are still there today. Days spent down by the river standing in the shallows and catching minnows or 'aeroplane' fish as we called them, in a glass jar. Watching the fish swim round the jar and eventually go inside, then lifting the jar out quickly and looking at what I'd caught. Taking the 'catch' home and wondering why it was dead the next morning and my dad saying 'why didn't you leave them in the river where they belong?' Days spent sneaking into the castle to climb about and not telling your mam and dad you'd been there because you'd get told-off! A freedom to go and play outside all day long in the holidays and your parents not needing to worry about you. Days when you could leave your bike outside and nobody would steal it! Days spent playing marbles in a grate or conkers while my sister played hopscotch or 'jacks'.

My dearest memories, though, were up Maltkiln Lane when there was a bowling green and a tennis court and I can remember a circus in the field between the two. Then after the tennis court was my hallowed piece of land – the village football pitch – I loved it there – the place where my 'heroes' played football every other Saturday afternoon. I used to go up there on a Saturday morning and help mark the pitch out with sawdust brought from the mill; and kick a ball about. A childhood spent kicking a ball about – bliss. Going home for dinner then back to the pitch for the game. Playing football behind the goals and cheering when someone scored for Harewood. Some Sundays the players would go up to the pitch for a practice and it was my chance to play with my 'heroes' for an hour or so. I think they passed the ball to me out of sympathy but I didn't care, all these people were larger than life to me and I loved every second of it. I'm pleased to say some of the players are still with me today. Thanks for the memories. As for me, I'm still in the throes of childhood and still kicking a ball about ...

The Ghost of the Harewood Arms

A few years ago a number of friends were having a drink (or several) at the Harewood Arms. One person, by far the worst for drink, said that he was going to the toilet. When he did not return for quite some time no one was in the least bit bothered as they thought he just decided to go home. In the very small hours in the morning the hotel staff were awoken by a great deal of noise coming from the cellar. As everyone was convinced that it was the ghost of the Harewood Arms, no one was quick to volunteer to investigate the source of the noise. Eventually, the landlord was goaded into having a look in the cellar. What the landlord discovered was not the ghost of the Arms but a rather confused and still worst for drink patron of the Arms. The landlord walked the 'ghost' home. To this very day, if this story is told in the Arms and the 'ghost' is within ear-shot, he still turns bright red with embarrassment.

St John's Ambulance to the Rescue

We have happy memories of Harewood (House) when we used to take our two grand-daughters every Saturday and spend the day there going round the bird garden, having our lunch at the little café or taking a picnic, going in the House and watching their surprised faces at the splendour of the gallery room, then finishing up at the Adventure Playground and always coming away with little gifts bought with their spending money from the gift shops, but one Saturday was very different. Our 10 year old grand-daughter (she is now 18) was enjoying the big slide but when she reached the bottom with a thud she cried uncontrollably and said she was in pain as she had heard something click in her back and couldn't (or daren't) move. We immediately contacted St John's Ambulance who was on site and they put into practice their routine for accidents, organised an ambulance, which came from Bramham, and took my grand-daughter to Harrogate hospital crying her eyes out all the way and scaring me to death. Every bump in the road seemed like a ride on the "big dipper" as she yelled in pain and I sitting next to her laid on the bed wishing it was me instead of her. After X-rays and first class attention at Harrogate hospital, whatever it was that clicked in her back seemed to have righted itself and after a night in the hospital we were allowed home.

We conveyed our gratitude to the St John's Ambulance staff who were glad their procedures proved a success as it was the first time they had cause to put them to the test and they were quite proud of themselves.

The Unpredictable River Wharfe

The River Wharfe has many moods from tranquillity to tremendous torrents. The River level can rise with great speed. There is a flood level of over a metre dated 1866 marked on the Mill wall.

Once we had to make use of our rowing boat to rescue pigs which were drowning in one of the piggeries. In 1965 I had a Labrador with eight well grown puppies in the stable and I brought them into the farm kitchen overnight as they were standing in flood water. I warned the children not to come down to breakfast until I had scrubbed the floor!

In a drought year a herd of bullocks waded across the water from the North side and disappeared into a field of maize eight foot high, and were not all found for several days.

The River froze solid for weeks in the 1970s and we and friends skated for quite a distance above the weir.

The Queen's Silver Jubilee

In 1977 during the celebrations associated with the Queen's Silver Jubilee, the whole village went down to the cricket field, where a sports day was held for the children and mothers and dads. Also, a cricket match between the village cricketers against their wives. Then a presentation to all the children of a commemorative mug and sliver coin. The entire village joined in.

The Village Cricket Team - 1

When the village had a cricket team my husband was a playing member and the wives used to make the teas and all the children played together in the adjoining field. The summers seemed longer and hotter.

The Village Cricket Team - 2

We used to do cricket teas – we had a rota and most of the young wives in the village took it in turns. My father, along with the rest of the family, was a very keen sportsman. Lots of people went to watch the cricket matches – my grandfather still went down to the cricket field when he was in his 80s. Back then we had a broken down old pavilion, not like the one there now. The old toilet was round the back.

The Opening of the Bird Garden and Memories of Stank

We came to Harewood in 1968 and lived in one of the flats in the stable block. There was no bird garden then, just garages. A short time later the bird garden was created and quite a few famous faces visited. Princess Margaret opened it. I remember her being very tiny. The tropical house was full of exotic birds and beautiful plants.

After five years we moved down to Stank where the farm was. Stank was like a little village on its own, everyone got on very well with everyone else. The children had plenty of freedom to play safely and lovely walks to go on from Stank. Lambing time and harvest time were our favourite times on the farm. Yorkshire Television came and filmed a few times at Stank and some of the farm hands took part when asked and again we saw some well known stars. We were all very sad when the farm closed down in 1984.

Swallows Remembered

Springtime and the swallows would arrive, soaring and darting, then through the bird-flap and into the old store shed. Nesting in the high beams, they were safe in the constant silence and twilight. Muffled sounds and twittering could soon be heard, and activity speeded up as fledglings trained for their long flights from The Avenue to Africa. Come a September evening, the swallows were smartly lined up on the cables. Gone by morning. The shed was strangely quiet but always awaiting the next season of swallows.

First Impressions

My first memory of arriving in Harewood in 1984 is the warmth of the welcome given to me by the villagers. Many of them had worked for the

Harewood Estate and they spoke with great affection of The Princess Royal, who often visited people in their houses, but were sad that the new generation did not play any part in village life. The majority of these people are now dead but their memories of what life was like in the village made a great impression on me.

A Golden Wedding Meal

During the war, Harewood House was a hospital for officers. The Gallery was one big ward and the big window from the gallery was opened for them to come in and out that way. They were very good. A couple met there and got married. They came back to Harewood to celebrate their golden wedding and had a meal in the café. I got an invitation because I was down there at the time. It was a very nice event.

The Frozen Lake

The lake in the grounds of Harewood House used to freeze over in winter but we couldn't go onto the lake until it was a certain degree. I remember someone cycling across it. I only used to skate a bit – I was usually the goal keeper and if I heard a crack I wanted to be off!

Lord Harewood and The Princess Royal used to skate with us on the lake. They were ever so good and we always had ladders in case the ice broke anywhere. The Princess Royal was a lovely person.

The Princess Royal and Guide Training

The Princess Royal paid for another person and me to go to the New Forest for two weeks training for guides/brownies. It was really lovely because there were people from abroad, all dressed in uniform, some of them were very wealthy. I remember there was a sister to a wealthy cricketer. We were all on the same level being dressed in uniforms, no-one was better than anyone else; it was really good, really lovely. Then we had to go to tell The Princess Royal all about it, she was more nervous than we were. She really was a lovely lady.

The Princess Royal and the Boy with the Paralysed Arm

There was a boy whose father was a shepherd or pig man. For years the man's son had a paralysed arm held by an iron bar. The Princess met him one day and asked what was wrong with his arm. He said he didn't really know, although his mother and father would know. She went to see them and they told her there was no chance of making it better but The Princess Royal arranged for treatment and he made a full recovery. She used to do things like that.

Attending a Royal Wedding

My favourite story about the Royals is when I went to this Lord's first wedding – all the Royals were there – we went to Clarence House for the reception. I enjoyed meeting all the people I never thought I would ever meet, e.g. Royal Family at the reception. Your name was called out as you went in. You were not formally introduced to them but you were just announced when you went in.

The invitation was for my mother and father, but mother was an invalid so dad said he couldn't go without her. He went back to the Resident Agent who had issued the invitations and said they should give the invitation to someone else – the Agent suggested me and I jumped at the chance. Although I had tonsillitis, I was determined to go. I only had a sip of champagne. It was a lovely event. My brother in law's aunty had a hotel in Russell Square so we took the Underground there and stayed until our train back to Leeds left at 3am.

A Stoll and a Box of Cigars

When it was the year (1961) of my parent's golden wedding the wife of the Resident Agent asked me to get the marriage certificate of my parents so that she could give it to The Princess Royal who in turn would give it to the Queen. On the day of the golden wedding a telegram arrived – a huge surprise for my parents as they didn't think the Queen would know about it. The Princess Royal gave my mother a lovely stoll and my father a box of cigars. I gave my parents a television set, only the second one in Harewood.

My Father the Headmaster

My father went to Harewood in 1915, newly married, to become head of Harewood School. When he went off to war in 1916 my mother took over the headship until my father returned.

Harewood was always a very good school; a lot of the children went on to Harrogate Grammar School. We were the only family (plus the doctor and vicar) who were not Estate workers. Father was once told by one of the teachers – the maths teacher at the Grammar School – that he didn't need to teach Harewood children any arithmetic until the third year, which was very good. My father was very sporty, a good cricketer and footballer and the children liked him. Although he was very strict, he had a great sense of humour. A lot of former students used to go back to see him. He was at the school until he retired at 65.

A Dedicated Man

The headmaster was a very good teacher. We used to go back to school at night and he used to give us extra coaching in various subjects, but particularly in maths. He did that after school for anyone who wanted to go and quite a few of us did. It was extra coaching for the entrance to Grammar School.

The Lascelles Boys

The two Lascelles boys (Lard Harewood and his brother, Gerald) were the same age as my brother and I. They went to Eton and when they came back for holidays, they had an old governess who came for the holidays. The boys used to drive round in a little horse and cart. We always felt sorry for them because it looked like a very lonely life. One year someone wrote to father before they came back and asked if he could get a boy's cricket team going – father actually coached them and they played a lot of the local villagers. Another year the Lascelles boys did a newspaper during the holidays – local news – it was something for the boys to do because it must have been very lonely.

Brigands Cave

One of the passages under Church Lane, used as a cart track from the South park to North park, is known as 'Brigands Cave' because in 1923 students from Leeds University, as part of their 'rag week' stunts, captured Princess Mary and held her captive for a short time in this underground passage.

Queen Mary

Queen Mary used to come and stay with Princess Mary every year and they always notified my father from the Estate when she was going home and they took the school children down to the drive, before the gate, and Queen Mary always stopped the car and got out and spoke to the children, which was always a very nice thing to do.

Playing Hide-and-Seek in the Castle

We used to go in and climb to the top of the castle. There was a beautiful sideboard in stone opposite the main entrance, beautifully carved. We used to go and play there and play hide-and-seek. One day a girl climbed to the top and fell off, I think she probably broke a lot of bones, but she survived. We used to walk from Church Lane through the woods to the castle, behind Bondgate, and pick the sweet chestnuts. Part of the joy of it was that the Head Keeper didn't like us being there so he chased us with his dog, which was a bit of a thrill!

Sledging - 1

There used to be an old farm in Bondgate (new houses are there now) and behind it was where we used to sledge. As this was near the top of Harewood Bank, we were able to sledge all the way down to the main road, but it was a very long way to walk back up. In those days there were not very many trees, they were planted many years later. As village children we used to sledge for many years.

Sledging – 2

I remember sledging. We used to sledge from the rough arch near the farm and sledge right down to the road. It was lovely going down but not so much fun coming back up. We also sledged in the top field in front of the bottom row of houses. We used to go down in a big old enamel bowl – we used to sit in that and go down and it tipped us out at the bottom. We also had home made wooden sledges – the blacksmith added iron to them for us.

I remember I went with a friend from the village and we sledged down from the field below the top field. I saw that there was some wire at the bottom so I jumped off the sledge and left her on. She wasn't very popular when she got back home and got into trouble because her stockings were ripped. She reminded me of it many years later!

Retiring in Harewood

When my father retired, The Princess Royal sent a message, via the Agent, to say that if he would like to stay in the village when he retired, he could buy a piece of land. It was a great honour because it was the first piece of land to be bought anywhere in the village, but he had been the Head for about 40 years. So father built The Bungalow opposite the school – the land there was actually the school garden – in those days in the country, the children learned a lot about gardening and producing things. We bought the piece of land, built the bungalow and were allowed to rent the land at the side which became the orchard, and the paddock (which is now The Mews).

All Saints Church

My father was the vicar's warden there for 40 years. We were all in the choir and went to Sunday School. You got marks which went towards prizes – 4 marks for going to Sunday School in the afternoon plus 6 for attending School in the morning as well.

The church used to be packed when Queen Mary came, it holds 500 people, very large for a small village, but people will have come from other villages. H H Griffith was there for a long time (1928 to 1974).

I was very lucky because when it came to my daughter getting married about 20 years ago, a friend who does a lot of work with parks in Leeds told me that you can get permission to be married in a redundant church. I rang London and they asked why I wanted it – in case it was for snobbish reasons – but I told them that the family attended there for years and my father was the warden there, so they said yes and she was the first one to be married there after it became redundant. They do have occasional weddings there now. At that time, they had been holding music concerts in the church so they had heaters and a red carpet and a message came from the Estate Agent that they would leave the carpet down for our wedding and also the heaters. A friend had a little organ in her house because the church organ had been taken out, so that was taken down to the church for the wedding.

Fondest Memory

This is a difficult one but certainly seeing The Princess Royal giving the prizes at school is one of them. This is a very happy memory. She was lovely, always very gracious. Another is the freedom we had as kids to walk round the Estate. We used to love it. Very happy memories altogether of the village and the children. We all got on well together.

A Sadness: the Village Hall

One sadness – yesterday when talking to a friend who is now in The Mews – and she told me that the Village Hall is now dilapidated. Collingham is thriving, has all sorts of committees and meetings. I can't understand it with all the new influx of people into the village, I'd have thought there'd be things going on. We raised the money for it and it was a beautiful building. We used to have dances, all in evening dress.

Queen Elizabeth II's Visit

When the Queen came to Harewood – a lovely bright sunny day. The dozens of policemen who all were very good natured and didn't tell us off for throwing kisses to the Queen, who smiled and waved at us – and Prince Phillip who thought it extremely funny. The Queen looked absolutely beautiful in her peach outfit. A wonderful day for everyone.

A Harewood House Volunteer

The last eight years I have worked in Harewood House – first as Mrs Bridges in the kitchens – and now in the State Rooms – it is a great pleasure telling the varied visitors (from all over the world) about the history and the wonderful art, both subjects I love. I have met some wonderful people, so it will always be an ongoing memory for me.

What a 'Pane'

I was at Harewood school and we used to go one afternoon into the garden and do jobs – the school garden was where the bungalow is now. We enjoyed it, getting out of school. This particular afternoon, I was sitting on the edge of one of the frames and a pane of glass broke. The headmaster said "You get your father to ask the joiner to get another pane of glass". The reply I got from my father was "If his head never aches until he gets that, he won't have a headache for a long time"! I was frightened to death, but nothing else was said about it and the glass was never replaced.

The Harewood WI

Harewood Women's Institute celebrated their 86th Anniversary in April 2005. It was formed just four years after the start of the Women's Institute Movement in 1915 so was one of the oldest in the country.

Harewood WI began when a meeting was convened on Tuesday 11th March 1919 for women of the village to discuss the forming of a WI. The Chair was taken by the late Florence, Countess of Harewood, Grandmother of the present Earl of Harewood. It was proposed that Harewood WI be formed, the first meeting to be held in Harewood School on Tuesday 1st April 1919.

A Committee was formed with the Countess being elected as President, a post she held for a number of years and by 1921 the membership had reached 100. Many of the members were employed by, and lived on, the Harewood estate.

The late HRH The Princess Royal was made Honorary President and honoured us with her presence on many occasions.

A WI is a place for learning and friendship, which I personally have enjoyed for many years. I have served as President, Treasurer and Secretary over the years of my membership and enjoyed the friendship of my fellow members.

It was with deep regret that Harewood WI had to close on 13th December 2005 due to the drop in membership. It is certainly one of my fondest memories.

Sports Day and the Work Basket

I used to enjoy sports day at the school which took place at the cricket pitch. All the prizes used to be displayed in Mrs Rhodes sweet shop (where the surgery is now in The Square – her husband did some tailoring behind the shop). We used to spend our pocket money there. All the prizes for sports day were displayed and I set my heart on this work basket, I think it was for the 100 yards race. I was determined I was going to win it, but I never got to the races because we were playing in the farmyard and there was a piece of wood which I trod on and got a nail in my big toe so I couldn't go! So, my uncle bought me a work basket – it wasn't quite the same, but I was very satisfied with it.

Cow Treacle and Mischief Night

When we were down at the farm, my father used to have molasses at the farm which he gave to the cattle – I used to call it cow treacle. On mischief night, myself and two others from the village (my friend and her younger brother), fetched a jam jar with treacle and went round painting the outside toilets (double outside toilets). It must have been my friend's brother who said, come on lets do it! No-one ever said anything, except for the people from the farm opposite – they went mad because we had put some on the gates! They didn't know who had done it but they were not happy! But we never heard anything about the outside toilets.

When we got back home my father caught my friend's brother and put lard on his neck and the soot from the kitchen fire which had gone out. His mother went mad because of the state of his white collar when he got home! My father didn't get us though! We got away with it!

School Prizes

Princess Mary used to come to school and present the prizes. I still have the prizes I was presented with by the Princess.

Courting in the Arbour

I met my husband when I was about 17 or 18 and he was about 2 years older. Courting – occasionally we used to go through the Pleasure Grounds, under the tunnel and sit in the "stony arbour". The Princess Royal used to sit in there and view the countryside. We used to go all over. We used to go to dances, we cycled to Huby, Weeton – that was before we got married.

Celebration Dances and the Annual Feast

We used to have celebration dances, e.g. a celebration dance after the war. We used to enjoy the 'feasts' in September. (A 'feast' is the name for an old fashioned fair with fairground rides, candy floss and so on.) The feast used to come once a year up to the war and then once after the war. I especially used to love the swing-boats and there was also the roll-a-penny and coconut shies. After the war the celebrations were very nice, everybody was glad it was over. I am sure there was a dance when it ended.

Climbing on Guns

I remember when the old field guns were in front of the gates to Harewood House, they were taken away during the war. We used to play on them, it was lovely. It was something to climb on. They were big guns with two big wheels.

Hopscotch in the Street

We used to have great fun playing hopscotch in front of the small houses between the garage and Scott's shop. We drew the squares on the path in chalk – no-one ever complained.

Home-made Ice cream

When the weather was good, my father used to make vanilla ice-cream. He used to put it in a big tub packed with ice and would sell it at weekends at the end of Bondgate.

The 'Serious' Business of The Harvest Festival

Shortly after moving to Harewood, I was invited to the Harvest Festival evening service, which is traditionally followed by an auction of the produce on display to raise money for church funds. This was the first time I met Olive Wild and many other people who have since become friends. The evening started of course with the thanksgiving service, followed by refreshments and then the 'serious' business of the auction started. Everyone joined in the bidding and the produce quickly disappeared. I successfully bid for some huge potatoes and other vegetables which had been grown by one of the villagers (which later proved to be delicious!). Olive was very keen to buy the marrow and had asked a friend to bid for her to make sure that she didn't miss it when it came up for auction. However, in her excitement and enthusiasm as the bidding progressed, she began to bid for the marrow herself – against the lady she had asked to bid for her! Despite protests, Olive would not be silenced and the two ended up bidding against each other – Olive won!! I was laughing so much I had tears rolling down my cheeks – what an introduction to the village! It's a pity more people don't support the local Chapel on a weekly basis, we really need greater numbers to ensure that the Chapel is able to continue in the long term.

Harewood Weaves its Magic

I have lived in Yorkshire all my life and visited Harewood House many times over the years. However, I had never really paid much attention to the village itself until I came with my partner (now my husband) to view a house for sale. As we parked on Church Lane, the sun was shining, the daffodils were in full bloom along the wall, and the vendor of the house greeted us at the gate like old friends – Harewood began to weave its magic and we knew instantly that we wanted to live here, even before seeing inside the house! It may not have the village community people describe of old, but we have made many friends, and it is such a beautiful area. Every day, we walk down the Church Lane bridle path and see the ever changing scene as nature reveals its splendour through the seasons – especially in Spring when everything bursts into life and the floor of the wood is carpeted with bluebells, the birdsong is wonderful and red kites soar overhead. When you get to the end of the lane and see the view across the valley, you can't help but feel your spirits soar.

Being Home and Coming Home (Author's)

I have lived all over the country, and spent many years living abroad, but when I saw Harewood for the first time, I felt that I had really come home. Never in my life have I ever felt so 'at home'. There is something very special about Harewood. Some of it can be explained in terms of the fabulous views over the River Wharfe, of Almscliff Crag and the striking Craven Hills; the abundance of wildlife – red and roe deer, red kites, song birds and so on; the wonderful walks in the area and around Harewood House; the peaceful churchyard of All Saints and the friendly villagers – but part cannot be explained. Let's just say that it is a 'feeling'. Also, no matter how far I travel away from my home, and the experiences I have gained elsewhere, I now never get the holiday 'blues' I once got. All I have to do is to walk down to the bottom of Church Lane and look at the stunning views and a smile comes over my face, for I am home.

CHAPTER TEN
A Selection of Harewood Walks

Sign for the 'Ebor Way' at top of Church Lane

Introduction

Below are three descriptions of walks in and around Harewood that I believe will give you a real feel for all that the area has to offer.

Walk One takes you for a short walk through Harewood village in order to see some of the wonderful buildings that have been built as far back as the 17th Century.

Walk Two takes you out of the village and down to the lovely River Wharfe and back via Harewood Bridge, past the area in which the toll bar riots took place in 1753 and returning to Harewood via the bridle path.

Walk Three takes you around the perimeter of the Harewood Estate and includes various views of Harewood House, the landscaping of Capability Brown, the grounds of All Saints Church and views over the wonderful Wharfe Valley.

I hope that with the map that appeared earlier in the book, and the directions given for each walk, you will have no difficulty in finding your way around the three walks.

Each walk is intended to 'stand alone' in terms of the information provided. Therefore, if you do all three walks, you will find that some of the information offered (for example, descriptions of buildings) will be repeated.

Walk One: Interesting Buildings and Architectural Features of Harewood
Time for the walk: approximately 30 minutes

This walk begins on Church Lane, which is also part of the Ebor Way.

The Village Hall is situated here and on the opposite side of the road is the development of Harewood Mews.

Walk on the pavement towards the top of Church Lane, where it meets the Leeds/Harrogate Road (A61) and turn right in the direction of Leeds.

The first point of interest, on the East side of the Leeds/Harrogate Road is the Harewood Arms Hotel that was built in around 1810. A fine example of Georgian architecture.

Just a few metres further along is the Primary School. The first school was built in 1768 by Edwin Lascelles, the then owner of Harewood Estate who commissioned the building of Harewood House in 1759. The old school was replaced by the current one in 1845 when the 3rd Earl paid for the new school and the Countess bought the books. Almost exactly opposite the school is a bungalow (called The Bungalow!). What is interesting about The Bungalow is that it was built on what was the orchard and gardens used by the school and is the first piece of land that the Harewood Estate sold. The person who bought the land and built The Bungalow was no ordinary individual. Mr Wadsworth was the headmaster of the school for 42 years and retired in 1956. Giving him permission to buy the land was a type of reward for services rendered to the village for such a very long time.

As you walk further along the road, towards Leeds, you will see to your right the first of two small square buildings that mark the entrance to Harewood House. The buildings are known locally as the 'pepper pots' (although they have also been referred to as 'pill boxes'). Believe it or not, people used to live in these one-room houses – with no hot water, a small scullery and an outside toilet. Walk on just beyond the first 'pepper pot' and stop for a moment to have a look at the Doric Arch that leads to Harewood House. A Doric Arch is typically a grand, imposing entrance. As mentioned in Chapter Two, the word Doric comes from the name of the fluted pilaster columns. (Another Doric Arch is Marble Arch in London, built by John Nash in 1828. It was the chief entrance to Buckingham Palace until the Palace was extended in 1851 and now stands as an entrance to Hyde Park and near Oxford Street.) The Harewood Doric Arch was designed by John Carr, the person who designed Harewood House, and was built in 1801 by a local stonemason John Muschamp. Cannons used to stand on the lawns on either side of the drive but were removed during World War II as their metal was needed for the war effort.

If you look in the trees above the second 'pepper pot' you will see one of the largest rookeries for miles around. It may not rank as an architectural feature, but the sheer size of the rookery is impressive nonetheless!

Cross the road leading to Harewood House and walk on along the A61, past the second 'pepper pot' until you come to a door in the wall, marked 'permissive footpath'. Go through and stop almost immediately to have a look at Ivy Cottage. This is the oldest building in Harewood and if you look very carefully at the lintel above the door you will be able to see the date – 1675. It is not known when the cottage became derelict or if there are any plans to either renovate it or to pull it down. In terms of additional information about it, Wade[i] said that it "probably was a toll bar/lock up and later was used as a keeper's house".

Go back through the gate and return the way you have just come past the Doric Arch and cross the A61 using the pedestrian crossing at the traffic lights. Once you have crossed the A61 you join a road called The Avenue (A659) going towards Collingham. Cross The Avenue so that you are walking on the South side of the road, the same side as the Post Office and Village Shop.

Just past the Post Office is the Anglican/Methodist Harewood Chapel. The

Chapel was originally the Literacy and Scientific Institute which opened in 1853. As mentioned in Chapter Two, when it was opened it was lit by gas and had an extensive library which grew to eight hundred books by 1859 and fourteen hundred by 1901. Lectures and evening classes were held, periodicals and newspapers supplied – even chess boards. The Institute closed when the Village Hall opened in 1959, although it was still used for storage of records until 1964 when it became the Methodist Chapel (the Methodist Chapel was previously at 5 The Avenue). In January 1977 the Methodist Chapel became the combined Anglican/Methodist Chapel it is today. For information, the Post Office and Village Store next to The Chapel have been there since the same time as the Institute, 1853.

On the opposite side of The Avenue, you will see a building with eight half moon shaped windows. This building was originally built by John Carr in 1755 as the ribbon factory. The ribbon factory only lasted for about eleven years. When the factory was closed the building was converted into flats, and that remains the case today. The building of the ribbon factory was just part of the grand scheme Edwin Lascelles had for the creation of what he called his 'model village'. All of the houses on the same side of the road as the old ribbon factory were built in the middle of the 18th Century. By contrast, most of the buildings on the same side of the road as the Post Office were built between the early and the middle of the 19th Century. Behind the Post Office you can still see a few of the outbuildings that were built behind many of the cottages along The Avenue – reminders of smaller industries that were here; cobblers, tailors, saddlers and joiners shops. Continue the walk past the Post Office and Chapel to the end of The Avenue.

The last house on The Avenue on the South side is The Old Vicarage (this was the Vicarage of Rev Griffith until his sudden death in July 1974). Cross The Avenue in order to get a closer look at the lovely buildings on the North side of the road. Proceed back to the top of The Avenue and turn right at the lights.

Walk back past the school and the Harewood Arms and stop just past the sign marked 'public footpath'. Once there, have a look at the two buildings at the top of Church Lane. These two buildings were also by John Carr. As you can see, the building on the right is a currently a furnishings shop called Jonathan Crawford. Over the years this building has been used for a whole variety of shops including Scott & Son grocers. Although the building on the left is now a private residence, it was once the village police station. Having a look at these two fine old buildings marks the end of this walk.

Cross the A61 carefully to return to your starting point on Church Lane.

Walk Two: Fitts Lane, River Wharfe, Harewood Bridge and All Saints Church
Time for the walk: approximately 60-75 minutes

The walk begins on Church Lane, which is also part of the Ebor Way.

Harewood Village Hall is on Church Lane and you will also see The Mews development opposite.

Walk on the pavement towards the top of Church Lane, where it meets the Leeds/Harrogate Road (A61). At the top of Church Lane turn left and proceed along the Leeds/Harrogate Road (also the Ebor Way) towards Harrogate until the end of the pavement. At this point cross to the other side of the road. *Be very careful as this is an extremely busy road!*

When you are on the other side of the road, continue walking along the road until you see a sign on your right for the Ebor Way, which marks the beginning of the walk proper. Proceed along the gravel path, pass through the gate and proceed down the hill towards the River Wharfe. This path is known as Fitts Lane. No one is really sure where the name came from but Ron Wade[ii] speculated that it might refer to low-lying water meadows in ancient times called Great Fitts which ran down to the River Wharfe.

As you walk along Fitts Lane you will see the remains of an ancient hedgerow. Continue along the lane until you get just about to the river, where the path you are on (Ebor Way) bears right. *Do not continue following the Ebor Way but instead turn left.* When you do so you will see a stile directly in front of you. Walk on with the river on your right.

Continue along the path until you come to the end of a fence where the path passes between a gap between trees – follow this path. As you walk along this lower path, closer to the river, you will pass by a fine stone chimney. The chimney was built as part of a proposed pumping station that was intended to draw water from the Wharfe. The idea was proposed by Leeds Corporation but the project was abandoned. Continue on the path past the chimney until you reach a gate.

Go through the gate and proceed for approximately 25 metres, then look left and you will get your first glimpse of Harewood Castle high on the hill (Harewood Bank). A bit further along you will get your first sight of

Harewood Bridge which was built in 1729 and was the site of the Great Toll Bar or Turnpike Riots of 1753.

As you walk along the river you will see various numbers on trees. These are the numbered places for members of the local angling club. Eventually the path drops down closer to the river and further away from the crops. Continue along this path until you reach the bridge.

Once on the bridge you will see a footpath sign on the opposite side of the bridge. *Ignore this.* Turn left, back towards Harewood. The buildings on your right as you come over the bridge belong to what was the old saw mill. The mill was sold in 1972 by Harewood Estate and the Earl gave silver ashtrays to all the mill employees to mark the occasion. Follow the pavement until you see a bus stop sign on the other side of the road. Cross the road at this point. *Be careful as this is a very busy road!*

After crossing the road at the bus stop follow the road to the right until you see a sign that says 'Church Lane', close to a pair of rather imposing wooden doors on the other side of the road (at the junction with the A659). Cross the road junction carefully and head to the wooden doors where the path continues. On the left hand door you will see an arrow indicating that it is part of footpath. Make sure you turn the handle on the door, do not attempt to simply push the door open. The sign next to the doors is 'Bar Lodge'.

Close the door behind you and walk straight ahead to the gate. The sign on the gate says 'deer with calves, keep to path'. Go through and continue following the well-marked path up the rather steep hill. At the top of the hill turn left and go past the cattle grid using the gate provided.

At this point you can do one of two things. You can either continue straight on along the Church Lane bridle path (Ebor Way) to return to Harewood village or you can turn right and go up the track to All Saints Church. If you follow the path to the Church, pass through the gate at the top and go into the churchyard.

The present Church was built in the middle of the 15th Century but the original one was built in 1116. Although access to the Church itself is only via the grounds of Harewood House, you can, nonetheless, spend a very enjoyable few minutes having a look at the exterior of the Church and the many fascinating gravestones in the churchyard. Depending upon the time of the year, you might also have the delight of seeing snowdrops, daffodils or bluebells. When you have finished with the delights of the lovely old churchyard, proceed back through the gate and down the hill to the cattle grid, turn right and follow the bridle path back to Harewood village. You will eventually pass through a gate at the end of the bridle path which marks the end of this walk.

Walk Three: A Walk around the Harewood Estate

Time for the walk: approximately two hours and the length is about five miles

The walk begins on Church Lane (Ebor Way).

Walk west along Church Lane, past the Village Hall on the right (Harewood Mews are on your left). Follow the path with walls on both sides and signed 'public bridleway'. This path opens up to show wonderful views of the Wharfe valley, as you approach the cattle grid.

When standing near the cattle grid, you will be rewarded with wonderful views of the hills of North Yorkshire, including Almscliff Crag, the majestic spire of St Barnabas Church in Weeton (built in 1851 and paid for by the Earl of Harewood); some glimpses of the River Wharfe itself and the Wharfedale Viaduct near Arthington, North Yorkshire. Yes, this is the same viaduct that appears at the beginning of *Emmerdale*. So, it is not just the stunning views that attract people to this particular walk, nor the chance to see red and roe deer, nor the abundant other wildlife including red kites, but also because of people's interest in seeing the area in which *Emmerdale* is filmed!

After drinking in the lovely views before the cattle grid, you might be tempted to turn left and walk up the short path to the ancient churchyard of All Saints Church. The present Church was built in the middle of the 15th Century but the original one was built in 1116. Although access to the Church itself is only via the grounds of Harewood House, you can, nonetheless, spend a very enjoyable few minutes having a look at the exterior of the Church and the many fascinating gravestones in the churchyard. Depending upon the time of the year, you might also have the delight of seeing snowdrops, daffodils or bluebells. When you have finished with the delights of the lovely old churchyard, proceed back through the gate and down the hill where you rejoin the road. Cross the cattle grid using the gate provided and proceed along the path, keeping the stone wall on your left.

When you are more or less level with a farm and the mill down in the valley, if you look to your left, in the woods (which used to be the Pleasure Grounds) you will see what looks like a temple. The 'temple' is a stone arbour and it, along with a stone urn, was added in the 19th Century. Until very recently, when extensive timber cutting took place in the old Pleasure Grounds, the arbour could not be seen. Jewell[iii] called this a 'rotundo' and described it as a majestic edifice with an elegant dome with one opening for the view of Almscliff and the other for the view of the Castle.

As you approach the brow of the hill, you get a very good view of the viaduct, the Church spire and Almscliff Crag.

The road eventually runs away from the wall and down quite a steep hill. At the bottom of the hill you will come to a four-way junction. Take the path to the left (although this is a continuation of the Ebor Way, it is not signed as such at this junction). The path continues through a field and on to another cattle grid. Once again, cross the cattle grid using the gate provided and proceed down the hill past farm buildings on your right and a lovely renovated barn on your left – Harewood Yard. As the renovation won an award, it is worth spending a couple of minutes reading what it says about the renovation on the large green sign outside the building.

Continue down the hill, passing through another gate – signed 'bridle way' and another signed 'Ebor Way'. When you get to the bottom of the hill you will cross over a small stream via a stone bridge. You are now in a place called Stank. After crossing the bridge the path takes a sharp bend left and then to the right to go up a hill in front of lovely old Carr house. Continue following the road/path until you come to another cattle grid and signed 'Ebor Way'. Cross the grid and continue following the path that runs beside a wood and eventually passes farm buildings on your left. Once you have passed the farm buildings you will be entering a wood.

After about 100 metres you will see a sign 'public bridleway' going to the right. Follow this path. As you proceed up the hill you will go past a telephone pole on the left. Approximately 10 metres past the pole the path takes a sharp turn left – up a steep hill. At the top of the hill you will join a number of paths. The path you want is the one that goes to the left which is marked 'public bridleway' and 'Leeds Country Way' (with an owl symbol). You will know that you are on the correct path if you pass another telephone pole on your left with the wires passing overhead.

As you walk along you will eventually see a number of buildings on your right hand side, through the woods, and on the other side of a stone wall. These are the buildings of the Emmerdale film set. As you continue walking you will be able to see the bell tower on the site. Please note that you are not allowed to leave the path and go closer to the set!

Continue following the path which then turns left at a sign marked 'Leeds Country Way' and 'public bridleway'. You will eventually come to a T junction and, once again, turn left following the same signs.

The path continues along and reaches a lovely stone bridge, which you cross. Once on the bridge if you look to your right you will see a number of waterfalls in the distance. Believe it or not, this wonderful stone bridge is simply called 'new bridge' and the waterfalls are simply wiers. The water flows into the fish pond you passed earlier at Stank. After the bridge, the path continues through a gate. Just through the gate, you will see a large oak tree on your right. Just beyond the tree, look to your right, across Grey Stone Pasture, and on the top of the hill is the large stone called Grey Stone. Grey Stone is what is known as a large glacial erratic boulder of Millstone Grit and is believed to date from the Late Neolithic and Bronze Age periods (2800 BC – 500 BC). As mentioned in Chapter One, I wonder if this stone gave Harewood its name? If you look to your left, above the tree line you will see Harewood House. When you get to the brow of the hill, beyond the trees, Harewood House comes into view again.

Follow the path through another gate. The path continues straight on for a short distance before turning sharp left at a sign called 'wall-side permissive footpath'. Go through the gates and follow this path that runs parallel to the A61. After just over a mile the path ends at the derelict house called Ivy Cottage. Take the time to look at the lintel above the door to see the date 1675, the oldest building in Harewood. Go through the green wooden gate and turn left along the A61 towards Harewood village.

As you walk along the A61 you will see the first of two almost square build-ings on either side of the gates to Harewood House. The buildings are known locally as the 'pepper pots' (although they have also been referred to as 'pill boxes'). Believe it or not, people used to live in these one-room houses – with no hot water, a small scullery and an outside toilet. After the first 'pepper pot' you will see the lovely Doric Arch that leads to Harewood House.

For your information, a Doric Arch is typically a grand, imposing entrance. As mentioned in Chapter Two, the word Doric comes from the name of the fluted pilaster columns. (Another Doric Arch is Marble Arch in London, built by John Nash in 1828. It was the chief entrance to Buckingham Palace until the Palace was extended in 1851 and now stands as an entrance to Hyde Park and near Oxford Street.) The Harewood Doric Arch was designed by John Carr, the person who designed Harewood House, and was built in 1801 by a local stonemason John Muschamp. Cannons used to stand on the lawns on either side of the drive but were removed during World War II as their metal was needed for the war effort.

After looking at the Doric Arch and the entrance to Harewood House, continue along the A61 past the Harewood Arms Hotel on your right, and a bus shelter on your left, until you come to Church Lane on your left, with a shop currently called Jonathan Crawford on the corner. This marks the end of the walk.

End Notes

i   Wade, *Vat Sal Be Sal* (1982), p 39.
ii   Ibid, p 8.
iii   John Jewell, *The Tourist's Companion of the History and Antiquities of Harewood* (1819), p 14.

Source Material and Bibliography

Allen, R E, *The Concise Oxford Dictionary of Current English,* Clarendon Press, 1990.

BBC Website, *Slavery and Harewood House,* c 2007.

Bogg, Edmund, *Lower Wharfeland,* James Miles, 1904.

Bogg, Edmund, *A Thousand Miles in Wharfedale,* Publisher Unknown, 1892.

Brewer, E Cobham, *Dictionary of Phrase and Fable,* Publisher Unknown, 1898.

Buckle, W H, *Harewood – A Guide for the Information of Schools,* Publisher Unknown, 1975.

Clark, Sir George, *The Illustrated History of Britain,* WHSmith, 1982.

Davey, John, *A Couple of Tours of Elmet,* A Ch4 Time Team Programme 1997, Downloaded from the Internet March 2006.

Dennison, E, and Richardson, S, *Harewood Castle, Harewood, West Yorkshire: An Archaeological and Architectural Condition Survey* (unpublished EDAS report for Harewood Estate), Forthcoming.

Gaunt, Arthur, *History, People and Places in Yorkshire,* Spurbooks Ltd, 1975.

GenUK, *Harewood – Topographical Dictionary of Yorkshire,* Publisher Unknown, 1822.

Griffith, H H, *The Story of Harewood and its Church,* Publisher and Date Unknown.

Harewood Estate, *The Heritage Plan,* Private Document.

Harewood House, *Harewood News,* January 1938.

Harewood House, *Harewood News,* August 1938.

Harewood House, *Harewood News,* September 1938.

Harewood House, *Harewood News,* April 1939.

Harewood House Trust, *Harewood A Guide,* Harewood House Trust Ltd, 1995.

Hey, David, *Yorkshire from AD 1000,* Longman, 1986.

Illingworth, John, *Yorkshire's Ruined Castles*, S R Publishers Ltd, 1970.

Ismay, Joseph, *A Visit to Chapel Allerton and Harwood in 1767*, The Thoresby Society, 1945.

Jewell, John, *The Tourist's Companion or the History and Antiquities of Harewood*, B Dewhirst, 1819.

Jones, John, *The History and Antiquities of Harewood*, Simpkin Marshall & Co, 1859.

Kennedy, Carol, *Harewood: The Life and Times of an English Country House*, Hutchinson, 1982.

Lascelles, George, *The Tongs and The Bones, The Memoirs of Lord Harewood*, Weidenfeld and Nicolson, 1981.

Leeds City Council (Planning Dept), *Ancient Monuments in Leeds*, Leeds City Council, 1985.

Linstrum, Derek, *West Yorkshire Architects and Architecture*, Lund Humphries, 1978.

Maidstone, Clement, *The Martyrdom of Archbishop Richard Scrope*, Translated with Notes and Commentary by Stephen K Wright (1997), Downloaded from The Catholic University of America website, May 2006.

Mauchline, Mary, *Harewood House*, Moorland Publishing Co Ltd, 1992.

Mercer, Derek, *Chronicle of the 20th Century*, Longman, 1988.

Routh, Pauline and Knowles, Richard, *The Medieval Monuments of Harewood*, The Kings England Press, 1983.

Schama, Simon, *A History of Britain 3000BC – AD1603*, BBC Publication, 2001.

Smith, Simon, *Slavery, Family and Gentry Capitalism in the British Atlantic: The World of the Lascelles, 1648-1834*, Cambridge University Press, 2006.

Wade, Ethel, *Wesleyan-Methodist Chapels*, Self Published, 2006.

Wade, Ron, *Vat Sal Be Sal*, Self Published, 1982.

Walvin, James, *The Colonial Origins of English Wealth: The Harewoods of Yorkshire*, Unpublished Paper, 2003.

Yorkshire Post, *Within these walls, a glorious past*, 30th July 2005.

Index

ABOUT THE AUTHOR

Although I hold a Professorship in Organisation Development, have a PhD, an MA and a BSc, strangely enough, I do not consider myself to be an academic – at least not in the intellectual, scholarly sense. In other words, I see myself as a down to earth, practical 'academic' who simply enjoys research of various types. I have gained just as much enjoyment from researching and writing this book, as I have when carrying out other research whether that is finding out about an obscure author of a book on leadership from the 1920s, or researching the life and times of Winston Churchill (my favourite 'Great Briton') or that of my favourite architect Frank Lloyd Wright.

But, when my head is not in a book, or my eyes are not staring at the computer screen whilst attempting to find information via the Internet, what else do I enjoy?

My favourite hobby is walking, especially fell walking in the Lake District, but I also enjoy walking virtually anywhere, as long as I can be in the out of doors. I certainly have a fondness for 'real ale', fine malt whisky, decent wine, and both cooking in and eating out. Italian is my favourite type of food. I very much enjoy travel (although not a great deal by car!), because I love exploring new places and experiencing all that different cultures have to offer. Yes, I even enjoy London! I have also re-discovered my interest in photography now that DSLRs are even better than 35mm cameras. I must have already saved a small fortune on all the film I have not had to buy and the useless pictures I no longer have to pay to get developed! I also enjoy gardening and do not even mind DIY. My various hobbies are made all the more special because my wife, Julie, shares in them – except drinking malt whisky, which she hates. However, I have not given up yet!

Finally, I became a Registered Volunteer with Harewood House Trust in July 2007.

Printed in the United Kingdom
by Lightning Source UK Ltd.
122851UK00001B/310-480/A